DESERT OR WILDERNESS

KEYS TO INHERIT THE PROMISE

F. Nolan Ball

Eyedentified Publishing Solutions | Springdale, Arkansas

Copyright © 2020 by F. Nolan Ball (posthumously)
All rights reserved. No part of this book may be reproduced in any written, electronic, recording or photocopying without written permission of the author. The exception would be in the case of brief quotations embodied in the critical articles or reviews and pages where permissions is specifically granted by the author.

Unless otherwise noted, Scripture taken from the New King James Version®. Copyright © 1982 by Thomas Nelson. Used by permission. All rights reserved. Scripture taken from The Holy Bible: King James Version. Springdale, AR: Eyedentified Publishing Solutions, 2020.

Although every precaution has been taken to verify the accuracy of the information contained herein, the author and publisher assume no responsibility for any errors or omissions. No liability is assumed for damages that may result from the use of information contained within.

Eyedentified Publishing Solutions
P.O. Box 6892
Springdale, AR 72766-6892

Book Layout © 2015 BookDesignTemplates.com

For inquiries, please contact The Rock of Northwest Arkansas at apostleballbook@gmail.com.

Publisher's Cataloging-In-Publication Data
(Prepared by The Donohue Group, Inc.)

Names: Ball, F. Nolan (Floyd Nolan), 1929-2018, author.
Title: Desert or wilderness : keys to inherit the promise / F. Nolan Ball.
Description: 1st ed. | Springdale, Arkansas : Eyedentified Publishing
    Solutions, [2020]
Identifiers: ISBN 9781945566172 (print) | ISBN 9781945566189 (ebook)
Subjects: LCSH: Trust in God--Christianity--Biblical teaching. | Ball, F.
    Nolan (Floyd Nolan), 1929-2018--Religion. | Obedience--Biblical
    teaching. | Deserts--Biblical teaching. | Inheritance (Christian
    theology)--Biblical teaching.
Classification: LCC BV4637 .B35 2020 (print) | LCC BV4637 (ebook) | DDC
    234/.23--dc23

CONTENTS

INTRODUCTION 1
WILDERNESS WANDERERS 27
WARNINGS ABOUT THE WILDERNESS 43
HOW TO RESPOND IN THE WILDERNESS 55
DESERT DWELLERS 65
WARNINGS ABOUT THE DESERT 85
HOW TO RESPOND IN THE DESERT 95
CONCLUSION 123

Acknowledgements

First and foremost, to **Shirley Ball**, Apostle Ball's wife of sixty-seven years. There was no greater inspiration and no greater love in the life of this great man than his beautiful bride.

To the **Ball family** for sharing their father, brother, grandfather, and great grandfather with countless numbers of people who were drawn by the Spirit to seek a safe place in Apostle F. Nolan Ball and The Rock of Panama City to realize and fulfill their identities and purposes IN CHRIST.

To **the ever-faithful people of The Rock of Panama City**. Apostle Ball was always quick to honor such a great people and a great house who made it possible for him to preach the gospel of the Kingdom of Christ around the world. Every message was tried and tested in and through the lives of people who yielded to the ministry of the Word and Spirit delivered faithfully week in and week out throughout forty-nine years.

To **JoAnn Jackson**, Apostle Ball's assistant for almost forty years. It would be impossible to measure the breadth and depth of her investment in Apostle Ball's ministry and the preaching of the Word through audio, video, print and in person.

To **Zoe Tatum** who tirelessly took the transcriptions from all the messages in this series and dovetailed them together into one manuscript. The ability to accomplish this feat cannot be overestimated. Zoe, your seed sown so many years ago is now being seen as a great harvest.

To **Maurice & LaTonya Jackson** who provided the service to bring the publishing of this manuscript into the book you now hold in your hands. (Eyedentified Consulting Services, LLC)

To **Todd & Autumn Murner** who had the vision to see this manuscript as a finished work so that many could be equipped and ready to traverse the prepared places in Christ.

To those **unnamed**, who aided in the dictation of these messages…. thank you.

Foreword

On Sunday afternoon, October 23rd, 1977, I drove into Tyndall Air Force Base, which is located on the east side of Panama City, FL. One month later, after being contacted by a friend from the Bible college I attended a couple of years earlier, I walked into Dirego Park Assembly of God church and had an experience that would impact the rest of my life.

As I walked through the front doors into the foyer of the church, I remember stopping and breathing in a smell I could only describe as "home". I then walked through the double doors into the sanctuary, down the center aisle and turned left down a row of seats under the front edge of the balcony. I had convinced four other airmen friends to come with me by telling them it was Thanksgiving weekend and surely someone would take us home for a home cooked meal (I was right and it was good).

Shortly after sitting down, a very sharply dressed, distinguished, white haired man walked over to us and put out his hand to shake mine and said in a deep, fatherly voice, "Hi, I'm Nolan Ball." It was a few years later when I realized what had transpired that day on Thanksgiving Sunday, 1977. I had walked into a house that would become my home and I had met a man who would become a spiritual father to me until the day he left his earthly home for his eternal home.

The book you hold in your hands is just one of the hundreds of messages that he heard from Father God and then delivered to the people that he loved so much and gave his life to for some 48 years. So much of who I am today as a father of three sons, a grandfather of ten grandchildren and a spiritual father to those who have been entrusted into my care comes out of walking with my spiritual father who was both a Pastor and an Apostle in my life for over 41 years.

So, as you read this book and decide if you are in a desert or a wilderness, I believe you will—by the help of the Holy Spirit and the words penned on these pages—know how to walk in the plans and purposes of God for your life victoriously.

George Brantley
Lead Pastor of The Rock of Gainesville
Gainesville, FL

Preface

The "Great Commission," which Christ assigned to His apostles and, subsequently, the entire body of Christ is fraught with many deviations. While many are looking for the straight and narrow path that leads perfectly to Christ's intended outcome, the development and maturity of each member of the body (discipleship) follows a course and process which may not necessarily be appreciated by others, seemingly on the same path.

Apostle Ball masterfully reveals a few rabbit trails, for which he is famous in his preaching, that one might experience through which Yahweh's original design and ultimate intention may be realized. While a majority of the "church" is looking to exit this world prematurely, Apostle Ball reveals Yahweh's nature of not forfeiting anything He created. Therefore, throughout one's journey through life, there are occasions by which a wilderness or desert experience will definitely become necessary and hopefully desired to preserve and manifest His plans and promises.

As you read through this manuscript of a preaching series Apostle Ball released many years ago, you will be fascinated to discover the desert and wilderness experiences of your past were divinely designed and initiated to redeem and restore all that rightfully belongs to Yahweh. Expect to breathe again in areas of your Christ life that may have been deprived of context and perspective. As Apostle Ball was famous for saying, "See again for the first time" a grand view of the kingdom of heaven, of which Christ is the KING, being established in all the earth, especially yours.

CHAPTER ONE
INTRODUCTION

I love the faith people. What a delight to be around people who have a positive confession! I enjoy being with those who call things that are not as though they are. I admire those people who are not moved by circumstance, but I have never yet met one person who with all of his faith, confession, confidence and declaring has been able to eliminate all the difficult places from life. Have you? I certainly have not.

However, what I have observed after decades of pastoring is that there are only two ways a person can get into trouble. That is right. There are only two ways someone can get into difficulty. The first one is disobedience. The second one is obedience.

Now everybody knows that the end result of disobedience is trouble and trials, despair and dismay. But obedience? How can obedience get a person into trouble? The answer is very simple. How many of you know that darkness and light are opposed to each other? How many of you know that the kingdom of the Heavenly Father and the kingdom of Satan are opposed to each other? When you set yourself to be removed from, translated out of the kingdom of darkness, and live in the kingdom of light, you are going to find tremendous opposition set against you. When someone becomes aligned with the purpose of the Creator, then he is out of alignment with the powers of darkness, and Satan and all of his demons do not like it. If Satan does not like Yahweh, why should a new Believer think for a moment that he likes him? The only time when Satan ever puts up with humans is when we are aligned with him. And when someone makes the determination, by the enabling of the Holy Spirit, that no longer will his life be directed by the god of this world and by his demonic spirits, the new Believer angers the enemy, and Satan sets out to destroy that person in conflict between the kingdom of light and the kingdom of darkness. Instead of flowing along with the powers of this world, the new convert has now turned around and headed against the powers of darkness. Immediately he will find himself surrounded by trouble. But his difficulty is brought about by obedience, not disobedience.

If a person is going to be in trouble no matter what he does, does it really matter if he is in trouble because of obedience or because of disobedience? Certainly, it matters. In order to respond correctly, a person must first discern the underlying cause of the trouble, because the proper response to finding oneself in trouble due to disobedience is markedly different from the proper response of the person who is in trouble because of obedience. In short, you will not know how to respond unless you know what got you into trouble in the first place. You see, if you are in difficulty because you followed Yahweh and obeyed Him, then when trouble comes, you should rejoice because the trouble is not found in you. The storm is not in you. The trouble exists out there, outside of you. The proper response to take in this circumstance is for the person walking in obedience to rejoice, rejoice, and continue rejoicing in the face of difficulty.

My brethren, count it all joy when you fall into various trials, knowing that the testing of your faith produces patience. But let patience have its perfect work, that you may be perfect and complete, lacking nothing. (James 1:2-4, KJV)

Surface reading of that passage would say, "Oh, thank Yahweh, I am in great trouble, so I am going to count it joy. It does not feel like joy, but I am going to count it joy." No, what James is really saying is revealed in the original Greek word for fall into. The word means to be caught between two opposing forces. It is used one other time in the New Testament to describe what happened to the ship on which Paul and the soldiers were being taken to Rome when it was caught where two seas met.

Any time you have two seas meeting, like at the southern tip of Africa or South America, turbulent waters are created, and it is a very dangerous place of sailing, especially in earlier times when vessels did not have the power or modern-day navigation controls. Even today, a vessel caught where two bodies of water meet is going to go through some difficult waters. We have an example of that principle being evident locally. Panama City is located on the Gulf of Mexico. We are blessed with numerous deep, natural bays that provide calm waters for swimming and other water sports. Some years ago, however, in order to ensure constant ingress and egress for the numerous boats and ships traveling to and from our Navy base, Air Force base, and local port, the Corps of Engineers dredged a pass through a peninsula jutting out into the gulf. All of the water going into and out of nearby bays and man-made channels flows through this one opening. Navigating the pass is tricky at any time, but especially when the gulf is choppy and the tide is high. The water from high tide becomes bottle necked in the bays and becomes turbulent as it rushes out of the narrow pass seeking the lower level of the gulf. If the gulf is choppy, then the vessel is caught between the violent water roaring out of the pass and the tempestuous waves surging toward the pass. It is a dangerous place. You can get into trouble there quickly because that is where two opposing forces meet.

And what James meant in this passage is that when you are walking in the will of Yahweh, when you are fulfilling His purpose in your life, you need to understand that you are going to encounter an opposing force. When the kingdoms of light and darkness meet, there is always a conflict. Nevertheless, if you find yourself in that situation because you are walking in obedience to Yahweh, rejoice. Do not panic, and do not turn around.

Follow the story of Yahshua through the gospels, and you will find that there was a constant conflict surging around Him. Born in the spirit realm, this conflict affected the natural realm. Spirits became involved in the conflict that the Savior created. The idea that Believers, that real Christians, do not create conflict just does not align with the word of Yahweh and does not align with the Messiah's life. Everywhere Yahshua went, unless He was with a close group of people who had allied and aligned themselves with Yahshua, there was always conflict. He could go in a synagogue on a Sabbath day, and demons would begin to cry out because of the pressure placed on them by the righteousness of His Father's kingdom present within Him. He created problems among politicians who felt threatened by Him, and His presence created turbulence in the natural world. How many natural storms were there that revolved around His presence? How many times in the testimony of the gospels do we read of storms erupting because of the presence of Yahshua and His disciples?

Wherever the kingdoms of light and darkness meet, there is always a tremendous conflict. When a Believer is walking in obedience, there will always be problems. Whenever you find yourself on the road of obedience, and circumstances erupt in your life because of your obedience, your response as a Believer should be what? Rejoice. Rejoice.

However, if you find yourself in difficulty because of disobedience rather that obedience, do not rejoice. The proper response for the person who finds himself in difficulty because of disobedience should be to repent.

For the sake of study and in order to set forth some scriptural truth, I have made a distinction between the place you go when you are obedient and the place you go when you are disobedient. I call the road of obedience the *desert* and the road of disobedience the *wilderness*. The Bible makes just such a distinction between the use of those two terms. But for the Bible scholars who will undoubtedly note that this distinction is not a rigid one, I concede that these terms—*desert* and *wilderness*—are sometimes used interchangeably in the Scriptures.

However, because there is a foundation for the use of these two terms in the Scriptures, let me give you this very simple definition. The *desert* is where Yahweh puts his followers, where they go because of obedience. It is a preparation place for something bigger and more important down the road. A *desert* is where Yahweh prepares His prophets, those who are called to the office of a prophet as well as all those who are going to be used by Him in other ways. Let me tell you, the desert is not a bad place. Yahweh's deserts are good places. You get there by hearing His word. You get there by obedience. You get there when you make a commitment to live out the word of Yahweh that has come to you—the dream, the vision, the prophetic word that has come to you. You see, when you are in the desert, no matter how difficult the struggle is, if you can look deep in your heart and know that you are there because of your obedience to Yahweh, you can rejoice, you can be glad, and you can take comfort in your situation.

On the other hand, a wilderness is the place that you go when you miss Yahweh's will for your life. It is a place of confusion, a place of wondering and wandering. It is a place of hardships, a place of difficulties. The wilderness is a lonely place. You do not even have the comfort of the presence of Yahweh's glory. You do not have the comfort of knowing that you are there in His will. Now in the Scriptures, especially the Old Testament, the wilderness of temptation and the wilderness of sin are usually used interchangeably. Generally, when the Scriptures refer to people being in the wilderness, they are talking about people who have missed Yahweh.

Now I have a good word for you if you are in a wilderness. Yahweh can turn wilderness experiences into deserts, but there really is no shortcut out of a wilderness. Even if, by the grace of Yahweh, you belatedly catch hold of His purpose, you are not guaranteed a quick exit out of the wilderness. Embracing Yahweh's will for your life guarantees you an exit out of the wilderness, but there may not be an immediately available exit. There may yet be a lot of wilderness to wander through to get to the other side. And what awaits you on the other side? *The desert, of course.*

Distinguishing between the desert and the wilderness is not an easy task however. Although the geologist uses those terms interchangeably, they are not one and the same in the spirit realm. There is a world of difference between a spiritual desert and a spiritual wilderness. What looks like the desert to some may look like the wilderness to others.

Difficulty looks like difficulty. The troubles that surround the obedient and the disobedient seem to be the same. The two vastly differing paths appear to the observer to be leading in the same direction. Yet the desert is Yahweh's preparation place for those who are in obedience, and the wilderness is Yahweh's detention area for those who have been disobedient.

Since the natural eye cannot tell the difference between a desert and a wilderness, you need to know what the criteria is for determining whether a place is a desert or a wilderness. The difference is established by *why* you are where you are. Did you arrive at this place because of obedience to Yahweh or disobedience to Him and His word to you? Once can you begin to understand how important it is to know whether you are in the desert or in the wilderness, then will you not know how to respond to your situation? If you do not know why you are in trouble or why trouble is around you, you will be confused about whether or not you are to rejoice or repent. And how you react, how you respond, to the desert or the wilderness ultimately determines how you are going to come out victorious or defeated. Because it is difficult to discern in the natural whether you are in a desert or a wilderness, you may be the only one who can identify exactly which path you are taking. Yet, your response is critical to what happens to you; if you think you are in a desert when you are in a wilderness, and you respond like you are in a desert, you are going to be in trouble; by the same token, if you are in the desert, you do not want to act like a person who is in the wilderness.

While most churchgoers view wilderness experiences as a routine, acceptable part of the spiritual learning process, I maintain that it is possible to walk all the days of your life in obedience. In the New Testament, Paul and Peter make similar statements that substantiate this position. They testify that the righteous need not walk in the wilderness. The apostles point out that Yahweh will make a way of escape out of temptation for His people.

> *No temptation has overtaken you except such as is common to man; but God is faithful, who will not allow you to be tempted beyond what you are able, but with the temptation will also make the way of escape, that you may be able to bear it. (1 Corinthians 10:13, NKJV)*

> *Then the Lord knows how to deliver the godly out of temptations and reserve the unjust under punishment for the day of judgement. (2 Peter 2:9, NKJV)*

Those who belong to the Heavenly Father do not have to walk the tempestuous road of temptation. He designed an escape route for them.

When Believers enter into the kingdom of righteousness, they are given a permanent *Get Out of Temptation Free* card. Peter learned about this benefit of the kingdom in the Garden of Gethsemane during Yahshua's final hours of freedom. The Messiah was involved in a tremendous night of suffering and confrontation and did what He was accustomed to doing; that is, He went to prayer and he invited the eleven disciples to go with Him. When they arrived at the Garden of Gethsemane that night, he then took Peter, James, and John a little farther along into the garden, as He also was accustomed to doing, while He prepared Himself to pray.

> *Then Jesus [Yahshua] came with them to a place called Gethsemane, and said to the disciples, "Sit here while I go and pray over there." And He took with Him Peter and*

the two sons of Zebedee, and He began to be sorrowful and deeply distressed. Then He said to them, "My soul is exceedingly sorrowful, even to death. Stay here and watch with Me." He went a little farther and fell on His face and prayed, saying, "O My Father, if it is possible, let this cup pass from Me; nevertheless, not as I will, but as You will." Then He came to the disciples and found them asleep, and said to Peter, "What, could you not watch with Me one hour? ***Watch and pray, lest you enter into temptation****. The spirit indeed is willing, but the flesh is weak." (Matthew 26:36-41, NKJV)*

Luke records this account in much the same way, except he relates that the Messiah urged them to use their Get Out of Temptation Free card twice that evening.

When he came to the place, He said to them, "Pray that you may not enter into temptation." And he was withdrawn from them about a stone's throw, and He knelt down and prayed, saying," Father, if it is Your will, remove this cup from Me; nevertheless, not My will, but Yours, be done." Then an angel appeared to Him from heaven, strengthening Him. And being in agony, He prayed more earnestly. And His sweat became like great drops of blood falling down to the ground. When he rose up from prayer, and had come to His disciples, He found them sleeping from sorrow. Then He said to them, "Why do you sleep? Rise, and pray lest you enter into temptation." (Luke 22:40-46, NKJV)

Now, Yahshua made a positive statement here about a negative situation. One of the things I have learned over the years from studying the Scriptures is that there is always a reciprocal of whatever statement is being made. The Bible seldom states both sides of an issue, but both sides are important and valid. Whenever the Bible provides a positive statement, there is always a negative, unstated declaration associated with the positive statement. Likewise, if you find a negative statement in the Bible, there is a reciprocal on the positive side. When you read the Bible, whenever you see statements made in the Scriptures, do not meditate only on the statement that is made, meditate also on the statement that is not made, the unstated reciprocal. Do not read only what is there; read what is not there as well, because sometimes what is not written is as revealing as what is written. If you only read what is in the Bible and do not comprehend the reciprocal of the statements in the Bible, you are going to miss about half of what Yahweh and Yahshua had to say.

In the passages from Matthew and Luke, the positive statement the Messiah made is that if you pray you will avoid going into temptation. The unstated, negative reciprocal Yahshua made in these passages is that if you do not pray, you will go into temptation; you will go into the wilderness. Knowing the trials that would soon be coming their way, Yahshua was pleading with His disciples and friends to pray so that they would not enter into temptation. He pointed out the fact that Believers had been given a *Get Out of Temptation Free card* and encouraged Peter, James, and John to use it. Since Yahshua encouraged the disciples to pray so that they could avoid temptation, it must be possible to avoid temptation, to avoid wilderness wanderings.

If it is not possible to avoid temptation altogether, to avoid those dry, barren places where we are separated from the Father's comfort, Yahshua was wasting some of his final precious minutes instructing His Disciples how to accomplish the impossible. According to the

Messiah, Yahshua of Nazareth, the only begotten Son of the living God, it is possible to avoid walking in temptation, walking the pathway of wandering, of wilderness. He never said it was an easily accomplished task, but He did indicate that the disciples could avoid temptation completely. If it is not possible to stay out of temptation, if it is not possible to avoid the wilderness experience, if it is not possible to be on time and on target with Yahweh, then Yahshua would not have made the statements He did in Matthew and in Luke. Yahshua said, "Pray so that you do not go in there." If Believers do not have to go in the wilderness, Yahshua would not have said, "Pray so that you will not." Again, the unstated reciprocal of the statement Yahshua made to Peter, James, and John is that if a Believer does not pray, he is going to enter temptation; he is going into the wilderness. If a Believer will pray, however, he will be able to discern the mind of Yahweh, and he will be able to avoid temptation.

So how do you avoid temptation, how do you avoid going into the wilderness? By praying! The *Get Out of Temptation Free card* is prayer and obedience.

Nevertheless, there is a school of thought in Christian circles that has been adopted. It is that believers must go through wilderness experiences, that somehow the righteous must go through torment in order to arrive where Yahweh wants them to be. And so often people will say, "Boy, you know I really learned a lot through that experience. You know, I thank Yahweh. It was hard to go through that horrible ordeal, but I praise Yahweh for it because it really taught me a lot."

If you really believe that the wilderness is a preparation place, why not ask Yahweh for an extended stay? Oh, no, Yahweh, I know my time is up but what about a thirty-day extension? Could I stay out here in this wilderness, puh-l-e-a-s-e? I have come to love the suffering! I have come to enjoy this hard place, Father. Oh, I like it out here! I am going to turn this into a vacation place.

No! Everybody that I know who is in the wilderness is always wanting to get out of the wilderness. Yet they are turning around and talking about how good it was out there in the wilderness, how much they learned out there in the wilderness.

You do not learn from wilderness experiences. You do not learn anything out there in the wilderness that you could not learn without going into the wilderness. Because, you see, what you learn of the kingdom of Yahweh comes by the revelation of the Holy Spirit, through the word of Yahweh. And you can get the word of Yahweh and the revelation of the Holy Spirit sitting, waiting on the Father.

It is not necessary that you go through wilderness experiences. Man does not learn from experience. Experience does not teach you one thing about understanding Yahweh. The only thing a person learns from experience is what he has learned or has not learned. It reveals what you already understood or proves to you what you did not understand. Experience does not add anything at all to your real understanding of the grace and the mercy of Yahweh. You see, experience is merely a testing.

If an engineer is testing a piece of steel, is he creating power in that steel? Is he creating weakness in that steel? Absolutely neither one. All the engineer is doing is proving what was already in the steel beforehand. His testing neither adds to nor takes away. Experience neither adds to your faith nor takes away from your faith. Experience reveals the degree or level of faith which you already had.

When you go for a driver's examination, does the examiner add or take away anything from your driving ability? No, he neither adds to nor takes away from it. He is simply there to examine what you already knew, or to reveal what you had not experienced and what you had not learned.

In the building trades, everything that is going to bear any kind of strength has been tested. Where they make concrete blocks, they must test them to determine how much pressure they will bear. And they test a block until it breaks because only then do they know how much weight it will really bear. But the testing process neither adds strength nor takes away strength. It only reveals. The character of that block, the strength of that block is predetermined by the ingredients in it and how carefully they were put together.

Let me share with you what I think Yahshua meant when He said, "Pray that you might not enter into temptation." It takes more than prayer, but Yahshua was saying that in prayer, we can discern a number of things about the will of Yahweh. What are some of the things that we need to know about the will Yahweh? Well, we need to know what. What is it Yahweh wants? Another thing we may want to know is *where*. Where does Yahweh want me to do this? When does He want me to do this? And who am I to be joined to in doing the will of Yahweh? And finally, how does he want me to accomplish this task?

You see, a lot of people know *what* Yahweh has called them to do, but they do not know *who* they are to be joined to (either marriage, in business, or in walking out their purpose); they do not know *where* Yahweh wants them to be positioned (geographically or in which church body); or they presume to think they know *how* Yahweh will accomplish His purpose in their lives. Nor do most Believers know when Yahweh wants them to move from point A, to point B, to point C, and so forth. So, they judge by man's timetable, thinking, "You know, I have been working toward this goal for a while now, and two years from now I should be where I am supposed to be. I am moving up this corporate (or spiritual) ladder rung by rung, and I am going to continue to move up until one day in the foreseeable future I will find myself on the rung of which I am supposed to be positioned."

No, when you have the prophetic word of Yahweh, you do not have to climb ladders. He may use that method to move you from the point where you are now to the point where He wants you to be, but He does not have to cause you to climb ladders. He can move you from the dungeon to the palace overnight. You do not have to advance as the unrighteous do. So do not think you know the *what*, the *where*, the *who*, the *how* or the *when*. Do not try to figure out *what, where, who, how* or *when* Yahweh is going to fulfill His word in your life. Do not limit Him by applying natural reasoning to His spiritual plans. If you do, you will miss His will for your life, and you will end up in the wilderness.

What you need is a specific word from Yahweh about His call on your life not just a general call, but a definite call. You need to have the prophetic word of Yahweh, and it will make what other people think is a wilderness Yahweh's desert for you, and you will be confident and comfortable there. You need to pray so that you do not enter temptation. You need to pray so that you will discern the mind and will of the heavenly Father for you in all your circumstances.

Let me share with you a principle I have learned. The Creator does not always deal with us in specifics. He does not always reveal His will to us through words of wisdom and words of understanding. Sometimes, He expects us to use natural understanding.

A few years ago, a family visited our church and really believed it was the will of Yahweh for them to move here to Panama City and to become a part of this church. There were a number of problems facing them. One major problem was that they had a house where they were living that they had not been able to sell, and they did not have a house here. They had jobs in this other city but did not have jobs here. Nevertheless, they had a desire to pull up stakes and say, "We will trust Yahweh."

Well, you can trust Him to do what He tells you He will do. But you cannot trust Him to do what you came up with. Wait on Yahweh. It is not enough to know *what* He has called you to do. You need to know *when* He wants you to do it. You need to know where he wants you to do it. You need to know with *whom* He wants you to do it. You need to know *how* He wants you to accomplish His purpose.

My response to this family was, Now, we are ready to receive you, and we are praying that people will come here. But if you do not have a job, my counsel is either wait until you get a job or until you have a sure word from Yahweh. Do not move on a general word that you need to move to Panama City. I come into agreement with you that you are to move here. But *when are* you supposed to move to Panama City? In my judgement, you do not need to move to Panama City until you have a job, until you have taken care of matters back home, and until doors are opened here, unless Yahweh says, 'Go, now!' Then you can go on the word of Yahweh, and I have every reason to believe that the job and the house and everything will work out when you get here.

Believers should not be presumptuous and then blame the Heavenly Father because things did not work out the way they wanted them to. Remember, Yahshua said, "Pray that you enter not into temptation." Do not get ahead of Yahweh. On the other hand, do not linger when He says, "Go."

Yahweh's timetable is somewhat like that little hole through which every satellite must be shot. Space scientists cannot arbitrarily decide when they will launch a spacecraft. The timing of each launch is controlled by some factors over which NASA has control, but it is also determined by some factors NASA cannot control. In order to put the space shuttle into its proper orbit, there is a small opening, a narrow time frame when a launch can be made. The launch can be made only during that small window of opportunity, or it must be delayed until the window is open again. Yahweh's timetable is not unlike this example in the heavens. For when a Believer misses Yahweh's window of opportunity, the window may never be available again, or it may only be available after a considerable period of time has elapsed. For the wandering Hebrews, that opening did not come for another forty years.

Failing to pay attention to Yahweh's timetable will cause Believers to be like the five foolish virgins in the parable of the ten virgins (Matthew 25: 1-13). The foolish virgins rushed off, unprepared. Five others were prepared and waiting. Now, in the natural, at first thought, we would probably think that those who were so eager, thinking, "We have got to go, got to go, got to go!" would have been the ones who entered in. But in reality, the five who waited and used that time as preparation time immediately entered in when the call came at midnight. They were able to join the bridegroom immediately.

There is timing of Yahweh's will for our life that is so critical, and so important, that getting ahead of His timing or missing it for whatever reason may mean forfeiting His purpose for your life altogether. You do not want to be in the bathroom when the midnight cry comes. You do not want to be saying, "Well, I need to pray." No, it is too late. Now is the time of preparation. Now is the time, wherever you are today in the will of Yahweh, to allow Him to prepare you for another visitation. Wait on Yahweh, and in your waiting, do not be overcome with slumber in the sense that you become inattentive to what Yahweh is doing.

Let me caution you. Most Believers who miss the Father's will for their lives will not enter into temptation by yielding to immoral, unethical, or unwholesome activities. Believers who miss Yahweh's purpose for their lives will do so primarily because they do not wait patiently on Him. They do not wait and become entwined with His purpose by discerning His ways and His time.

But waiting on Yahweh is not as easy as it sounds. It is difficult for other people to accept that you have heard from the Creator of all that exists and that you are merely waiting on further instructions from Him. It is difficult for your family; it is difficult for your friends. They say, "You must do *something*."

Let me tell you that waiting on Yahweh is doing something. It is not being irresponsible; it is not running from responsibility. Waiting on Yahweh is *receiving* the responsibility to discern the mind of the Creator. After all, can you imagine Yahweh running around helterskelter wondering, "Oh, my, oh my, oh my, *whatever* will I do?" Can you imagine the Heavenly Father ever wringing His hands thinking, "I do not know what to do! I simply do not know what to do!" Well, what you and I want to do is what He would do if He were in our shoes, right? We want to respond as He would respond. We want to say exactly what He would say. Therefore, we must learn to wait.

Let me give you a good rule if you do not know it. When you find yourself in a difficult place, sit down. Literally, if you find yourself in a distressing, emotionally disturbing situation, one of the smartest things you can do is to physically sit down. Avoid the temptation to be running frantically, going here and there, and calling this person and that person. Get yourself together! That is part of what it means to wait on Yahweh. When I have found myself in those distressing situations, people have asked, "What are you going to do? What are you going to do?" My response is, "I am not going to do anything but pray, and I am going to wait. And *when* I find out what I should do, what I ought to do, *then* I will do something. Until then, I am not doing anything."

Sitting down and waiting until you hear from Yahweh will also help you learn to get your body, spirit and emotions under control. So, sit down! And shut up. Quit running off at the mouth. You will create more problems, create more trouble for yourself if you do not sit down and shut up. Eventually if you are ever going to get out of the distressing situation, you are going to have to get the word of Yahweh into your spirit. So, wait. Wait. Wait. Wait on Him.

Believers are not called to success as the world counts success. What is success? It is knowing the mind and the will of the Father and doing that. That is success. And if Yahweh says wait, then wait. Somehow Believers have bought into the idea that there is some value in being busy. Busyness itself is thought to be something akin to a virtue. Yet, Yahweh will reward you for waiting, if waiting is in His will, and He will not reward you for running (being busy but producing nothing of spiritual value) if running is not in His will. You can go ahead and run, and you are going to grow more frustrated and farther away from the Father, and farther away from the answer. So, learn to wait on Yahweh. And keep in mind that there is far more value in waiting, when waiting is His will, than there is value in baseless busyness.

I do not understand people who talk about getting "burned out" serving Yahweh. You can get burned out on religion, but you cannot get burned out on the living God. You can get burned out trying to meet someone's expectations of what you should do but you cannot get burned out walking in the Spirit. Absolutely impossible! To say that you are walking in the Spirit and are burned out would be making a lie of everything the Creator is because there is no place more relaxed, no place more renewing, than to be in the Spirit of the eternal Father. Walking in the Spirit means when you are not busy with an obvious task, you are not necessarily idle. It means that you are busy maintaining relationship, communication, and fellowship with the Creator so that at the exact moment when He says, "Move," guess what? You are ready to move. You are not off somewhere chasing somebody's cat. When the moment comes, you are ready to go. Behold, the cry comes, "Go out to meet Him," and you are ready to go. But you are not moving at every voice in the dark. You are waiting on Yahweh because you have made up your mind you are not going into temptation. You are going to walk in His timetable by His Spirit, in His ways, to become His glory in the earth. You are not going to be moved. You are not going to become impatient. You are not going to become impulsive. You are going to wait on Yahweh. Others may ask,

"What are you doing?"

"Waiting."

"You do not have anything to do?"

"Yeah, I have a lot to do. I am waiting. I am fellowshipping. I found out my heavenly Father pays just as much for waiting as he does for running."

When believers run to and fro like chickens with their heads chopped off, they cannot hear their Father. They cannot be sensitive. They cannot be ready. So, learn to wait on Yahweh.

If we go through wilderness wanderings, it is not Yahweh's fault. If we go through complex, confusing times, it is not Yahweh's fault. If we are wandering forty years more or less in the wilderness, it is because we missed Yahweh. The wilderness is not His plan. It is not His purpose for our lives.

It is not Yahweh's purpose that young people go through wilderness wanderings either. Parents need to learn how to be a prophet or prophetess to their children. Parents need to learn how important it is to set the course and direction of their children's lives. They need to learn how important it is to know how to put their children into Yahweh's deserts and keep them out of the Devil's wilderness. Sowing oats, having a wild fling or teenage rebellion is not in the plan and purpose of Yahweh. But many young people are going through those experiences because the Church has come to believe that wilderness wanderings are the normal course of life. They may be for Ishmaels but they are not for the Isaacs and they are not for the Johns. Wandering in the wilderness is not for those whose parents have discerned by the Spirit of Yahweh His call and purpose as they prophesy the direction and will of Yahweh setting boundaries for their boys and girls. I tell you that young people can walk through the teenage years and they can stay out of the wilderness and they can abide in Yahweh's deserts in His preparation places.

Teenagers and young people need to learn to resist the world and anybody who wants to put upon them plans that are contrary to the Father's will for their lives. Yahweh has a plan, a purpose for every person's life. Every person needs to learn to wait on the Heavenly Father to reveal His plan. Yahweh will reveal His plan to those whom He has chosen regardless of age or experience. Young people do not have to run down a lot of dead-end streets and come back saying, "I wonder why I went down that road?" I am persuaded that from birth a person can walk out the perfect will of the Father for his life, and the road of life does not require wilderness experiences or wandering in circles. But the means to avoid wilderness experiences and temptations that lead away from the Father's perfect will is found in the *Get Out of Temptation Free card* – prayer. Regardless of age, in order to avoid temptation and being led astray from the Father's perfect will for your life, you must pray. And you must obey.

Because the truth of the matter is: those of us in the ministry are wasting our time talking to you if you do not pray. I cannot tell you if it is wisdom for you to get a cup of cold water if you are not a person of prayer. I cannot keep you out of the wilderness. I cannot give you enough wisdom. I cannot counsel you enough to keep you out of wilderness places if you do not obey the word of Yahweh. Quit looking for some magician, some prophet, to give you a word. I have a prophetic word from Yahweh for you. Get up and pray! That is a prophetic word. You can build your life on that. Yahshua said if you will pray, you do not have to go into the wilderness. You do not have to go into those hard places. Forget about burning bushes. Brother, when you learn to walk by the word of Yahweh, you will not need any burning bushes. Yahweh may give you one as a special, added feature, but you will not need it if you will begin to pray. There is nothing more important, nothing so urgent for you to do that you cannot set yourself to pray.

There are people in my church today who have gone through calamity after calamity after calamity. But in every case where I have seen those people commit themselves to intercessory prayer, I *have seen* and *am seeing* a tremendous release of the blessing, the anointing and the corrective power of Almighty Yahweh. Pray that you enter not into temptation. Pray! Seek Yahweh! Be diligent! And wait on Him. Your Father in Heaven will bring not only the knowledge of His will, but He will give you a knowledge of the right time, and He will give you the knowledge of how, and He will give you the knowledge of who and where. His plan will fit together so beautifully. You will not have to take a crowbar and force one thing into place. You will not have to take a carpenter's plane and shape anything; it will all fit together. There is a beautiful, simple statement made in regard to the building of the Temple of Yahweh in Jerusalem (Solomon's temple). Now that temple was made of probably thousands of huge stones. Individually, some of those stones weighed tons. Some of them were fourteen or fifteen feet long and stood three or four feet high and were just as wide. The temple was made of these large stones, gold, silver, and a lot of other materials. Yet, the Bible relates that the sound of the hammer and the saw was not heard in the building of the temple. Yahweh so ordained, He so fashioned, He so anointed that the whole temple was put together easier than a little boy putting his Lego blocks together. Yahweh's plan for your life is no less complex than His plan for the temple yet it is simple and all of the parts will come together peacefully. He has designed a magnificent plan for every individual's life, but in order to erect the building of purpose, each person must follow the plan He is given. Yahweh's instructions on how to build the building according to His specifications is to pray so that you will not yield to temptation so that you will not be distracted.

You know, I do not need burning bushes. I do not need shaking ground. I do not need flashes of lightening. I do not need voices that go, "Peep, peep," in the night. I do need somebody to give me a word because I have set my heart to wait on Yahweh. No one is pressuring me. No one is going to cause me to move from this place of rest I have

Desert or Wilderness

found waiting on my Heavenly Father's voice. I am not moving until I have waited on Yahweh, until I have discerned the mind of Yahweh.

You see, I have been in the wilderness before and I have seen a few burning bushes but they are no special attraction to me because I know where you have to go to see them. I know where you have to go to experience them and I would rather bypass them. Sometimes when I am traveling on a long trip, I see interesting places but I do not want to be sidetracked or delayed because I always have a purpose in my trips. I am on a journey. I have a destination and I do not have time or interest to stop and see all the tourist sites.

Yahweh has called the Church to a high and holy calling. He has a purpose, a call on every individual's life. Each of us was born with a purpose for their lives and Yahweh wants to lead us on a straight path. He wants us to stay out of the wilderness.

Now, my intention is to never spend one day, not one hour, in the wilderness again. One of the reasons I am diligent in prayer is because I do not like the wilderness. If I am going to be fighting the devil, I want to be fighting him on my terms and on my turf. I do not want to be out there in the wilderness without Yahweh's protection. I want to be out in the desert knowing that the angels of Yahweh are encamping about me, ministering to me the same way they ministered to Yahshua. I want to know that I am not forsaken but that I am surrounded, undergirded and watched over by Yahweh Almighty. Therefore, I am not afraid of any plague or anything that comes near my dwelling. It is not going to touch me because I am abiding in Yahweh.

And I abide in Him by hearing and doing His word according to John 15.

When you are in trouble, you need to know where you are. Are you in the desert or are you in the wilderness? You need to know why you are there. If you are where you are because of obedience, then you are in the desert. It is Yahweh's preparation place and it does not matter what it looks like to anyone else. Your Heavenly Father is preparing you for something bigger and better down the road.

All believers certainly believe that the Savior spoke the truth. He is the truth so obviously He spoke truth. Therefore, when He said, "Pray that you enter not into temptation," there are two obvious points we need to understand from that statement. One is if we do not pray, we *will* go into temptation and the flip side of that is if we do pray, we *will* not go into temptation.

And that is one of the purposes of this message, to help you to understand that you do not have to go into the wilderness. Yahshua went into the wilderness for you so that you no more have to go into the wilderness experiences than you have to go to the cross. If you do not have to go to the cross, then you do not have to go into wilderness experiences. If you do not have to go into the Garden of Gethsemane, you do not have to go through breaking experiences in this life.

No, there is only one way, only one way that you and I learn the things that we need to know. There is only one way that we become what we need to be. And Yahweh made it so simple. Unfortunately, man has come along with his religious thinking and has tried to make everything relating to Yahweh tremendously difficult. The Bible says in Isaiah that Yahweh will make a way and mark it and make it so clear and so simple that though a man were a fool, he will not err therein. Yahweh never makes His ways difficult. He never makes His way confusing. He never makes His ways complex. Always look for the simple. Always look for the direct. If it looks as if you are in a maze, you are searching and trying to find the grace of Yahweh, trying to find the wisdom of Yahweh – you got locked into a religious box. You got lost among people. It is people, especially religious people, who come along and make the things of Yahweh complex. Some people will tell you that the things of Yahweh, His word, and His Spirit are so complex that only a very few, special people could ever begin to understand Him. And only those special people after much training in schools and seminaries are qualified to begin to explain the works of Yahweh. That just simply is not so. Yahweh's ways are not complex. They are simple. His ways are not like wandering through a maze trying to find your way out. Yahweh's ways are direct.

He will direct your steps all the days of your life if you use your *Get Out of Temptation Free card* – prayer. If you pray, you can avoid temptation and you can avoid wilderness wanderings.

CHAPTER TWO
WILDERNESS WANDERERS

The truth of the matter is every one of us has been in the wilderness. However, our generation is not the first to be marked by wilderness wanderings. Many of our Biblical ancestors found themselves deep in the wilderness at one point or another in their lives. Nor do we have to get far into the Scriptures to find wilderness wanderers.

Abraham, the great patriarch of the Jewish faith, and Sarah, his wife, became wilderness wanderers. Abraham was called of Yahweh to leave idol worship and follow the voice of the unknown god into a land that this unknown god would show him. Yahweh promised to prosper Him and give him that land for an inheritance. Abraham realized that if he were going to leave an inheritance, he must have a descendent to receive it. In time, Yahweh gave him the promise that he would have a son by his wife Sarah. However, both Abraham and Sarah became a little weak and weary in waiting on Yahweh and devised a plan born of the flesh. Sarah suggested to Abraham that he father a son by Hagar, Sarah's handmaiden. About thirteen years later,

Yahweh gave Sarah the promised son of the inheritance, Isaac. Then Hagar became hated and despised in Sarah's eyes and her son Ishmael came to despise Isaac.

Now the real reason I believe that Ishmael was rejected of Yahweh is because he had no respect for the man of faith. He had no respect for the son of promise. For Ishmael, according to the Scriptures, began to ridicule and make fun of little Isaac. No doubt he resented Isaac and he ridiculed the idea that Isaac would ever take the place of Abraham's firstborn. I believe that it was his ridicule, his sarcastic attitude of unbelief and rejection toward Isaac that caused the break in the family and caused Yahweh to give instructions that Hagar and Ishmael were to be cast out of Abraham's family and rejected. Notice now what happened in chapter 21 of Genesis, verses 17-20:

> *And God heard the voice of the lad. Then the angel of God called to Hagar out of heaven, and said to her, What ails you, Hagar? Fear not, for God has heard the voice of the lad where he is. Arise, lift up the lad and hold him with your hand, for I will make him a great nation. And God opened her eyes, and she saw a well of water. Then she went and filled the skin with water and gave the lad a drink. So, God was with the lad;* **and he grew and dwelt in the wilderness and became an archer.**

He became a man of war. It is significant to me that Yahweh found the lad in the wilderness and it was there in the wilderness that he grew and it was in the wilderness that he became a hunter. So, figuratively Ishmael was born in the wilderness because Abraham was wandering in the wilderness when he entered into temptation to conceive him outside of Yahweh's revealed word. Then, Ishmael became a wilderness wanderer himself. And finally, he joined himself to a wife from Egypt, a nation that is itself a symbol of the wilderness.

Numerous political and religious issues that continue to plague the world in our generation are found in Ishmael's conception, maturing, and marrying. Israel, of course, is fighting and dealing with the sons of Ishmael even today, and the real threat of the Church is what it has always been. It is the counterfeit faith adhered to by Ishmael's descendants, the Muslim faith, for joined together in the Islamic religion is a belief in a supreme being and in an absolute political system. Thus, the Church's real enemy and Israel's natural enemy, is one born in, educated in, developed in, and wed in the wilderness, not in the desert place. Yahweh was not preparing Ishmael to be a ruler over His people because Ishmael had with sarcastic unbelief rejected Yahweh's anointed one. And once Yahweh's anointed one is rejected, there is only one other course to follow for an individual, for a family, or for a nation.

Another great leader of the Jewish faith, Moses, also went into the wilderness." Why did Moses go into the wilderness? Was it Yahweh's will? Believers often hear the explanation, "Yahweh wanted to shape him, so he sent him into the wilderness for many years." No. Moses went into the went into the wilderness because he did not discern Yahweh's times.

He knew what Yahweh wanted him to do and that was about all he knew Yahweh wanted. He did not know how he was to do it. He did not know when he was to do it. He did not know who was to join him in it. Let us look at the passages in Exodus that pertain to Moses' wilderness wanderings.

> *Now it came to pass in those days, when Moses was grown, that he went out to his brethren and looked at their burdens. And he saw an Egyptian beating a Hebrew, one of his brethren.*
>
> *So, he looked this way and that way, and when he saw no one, he killed the Egyptian and hid him in the sand.*
>
> *And when he went out the second day, behold, two Hebrew men were fighting, and he said to the one who did the wrong, "Why are you striking your companion?"*
>
> *Then he said, "Who made you a prince and a judge over us? Do you intend to kill me as you killed the Egyptian?" So, Moses feared and said, "Surely this thing is known!"*
>
> *When Pharaoh heard of this matter, he sought to kill Moses.* **But Moses fled from the face** *of Pharaoh and dwelt in the land of Midian; and he sat down by a well.*
>
> *Now the priest of Midian had seven daughters. And they came and drew water, and they filled the troughs to water their father's flock.*
>
> *Then the shepherds came and drove them away; but Moses stood up and helped them and watered their flock.*
>
> *When they came to Reuel [Jethro], their father, he said, "How is it that you have come so soon today?"*

And they said, "An Egyptian delivered us from the hand of the shepherds and he also drew enough water for us and watered the flock."

So, he said to his daughters, "And where is he? Why is it that you have left the man" Call him, that he may eat Bread."

Then Moses was content to live with the man, and he

gave Zipporah his daughter to Moses.

And she bore him a son and he called his name Gershom; for he said, "I have been a stranger in a foreign land."

Now it happened in the process of time that the king of Egypt died. Then the children of Israel groaned because of the bondage and they cried out and their cry came up to God because of the bondage.

So, God heard their groaning and God remembered his covenant with Abraham, with Isaac, and with Jacob. And God looked upon the children of Israel, and God acknowledged them (Exodus 2:11-25, NKJV).

Now Moses kept the flock of Jethro his father-in-law, the priest of Midian. And he led the flock to the back of the desert, and came to Horeb, the mountain of God.

And the Angel of the Lord appeared to him in a flame of fire from the midst of a bush. So, he looked and behold, the bush burned with fire but the bush was not consumed.

The Moses said, "I will now turn aside and see this great sight why the bush does not burn."

So, when the Lord saw that he turned aside to look, God called to him from the midst of the bush and said, "Moses, Moses!" And he said, "Here I am."

Then He said, "Do not draw near this place. Take your sandals off your feet, for the place where you stand is holy ground."

Moreover, He said, "I am the God of your father – the God of Abraham, the God of Isaac, and the God of Jacob." And Moses hid his face, for he was afraid to look upon God.

And the Lord said: I have surely seen the oppression of My people who are in Egypt, and have heard their cry because of their taskmasters, for I know their sorrows;

So, I have come down to deliver them out of the hand of the Egyptians, and to bring them up from that land to a good and large land, to a land flowing with milk and honey, to the place of the Canaanites and the Hittites and the Amorites and the Perizzites and the Hivites and the Jebusites.

Now therefore, behold, the cry of the children of Israel has come to Me, and I have also seen the oppression with which the Egyptians oppress them.

Come now, therefore, and I will send you to Pharaoh that you may bring My people, the children of Israel, out of Egypt. (Exodus 3:1-10 NKJV)

And the Lord said to Aaron, "Go into the wilderness to meet Moses." So, he went and met him on the mountain of God and kissed him. (Exodus 4:27, NKJV)

"So, we departed from Horeb, and went through all that great and terrible wilderness which you saw on the way to the mountains of the Morites, as the Lord our God had commanded us. Then we came to Kadesh Barnea.

And I said to you, 'You have come to the mountains of the Amorites, which the Lord our God is giving us.

Look, the Lord your God has set the land before you; go up and possess it, as the Lord God of your fathers has spoken to you; do not fear or be discouraged.'

And every one of you came near to me and said, 'Let us send men before us, and let them search out the land for us, and bring back word to us of the way by which we should go up, and of the cities into which we shall come.'

And the plan pleased me well; so, I took twelve of your men, one man from each tribe.

And they departed and went up into the mountains, and came to the Valley of Eshcol, and spied it out.

They also took some of the fruit of the land in their hands and brought it down to us; and they brought back word to us, saying, 'It is a good land which the Lord our God is giving us.'

Nevertheless, you would not go up, but rebelled against the command of the LORD your God:

And you murmured in your tents, and said, 'Because the LORD hates us, He has brought us out of the land of Egypt to deliver us into the hand of the Amorites, to destroy us.

Where can we go up? Our brethren have discouraged our hearts, saying, "The people are greater and taller than we; the cities are great and fortified up to heaven; moreover, we have seen the sons of the Anakim there."

Then I said to you, 'Do not be terrified, or afraid of them.

The LORD your God, who goes before you, He will fight for you, according to all He did for you in Egypt before your eyes;

And in the wilderness where you saw how the Lord your God carried you, as a man carries his son, in all the way that you went until you came to this place.'

Yet, for all that, you did not believe the LORD your God, who went in the way before you to search out a place for you to pitch your tents, to show you the way you should go, in the fire by night and in the cloud by day.

And the LORD heard the sound of your words, and was angry, and took an oath, saying, 'Surely not one of these men of this evil generation shall see that good land of which I swore to give to your fathers.

Except Caleb the son of Jephunneh; he shall see it, and to him and his children I am giving the land on which he walked, because he wholly followed the Lord.

The LORD was also angry with me for your sakes, saying, 'Even you shall not go in there; but Joshua the son of Nun, who stands before you, he shall go in there.

Encourage him, for he shall cause Israel to inherit it. Moreover, your little ones and your children, who you say will be victims, who today have no knowledge of good and evil, they shall go in there; to them I will give it, and they shall possess it. **But as for you, turn and take your journey into the wilderness by the Way of the Red Sea.'** *(Deuteronomy 1:19-40, NKJV)*

Moses unequivocally missed it. I am persuaded that Moses knew what Yahweh wanted him to do, but he failed to wait on Him for the revealing of His time and His way. In acting prematurely, he got ahead of the Heavenly Father. And he ended up in the wilderness because he had to run for his life. When Moses slew the Egyptian, Yahweh was not yet ready to deliver the Hebrews from Egypt, and Yahweh was not going to change His timetable for an impetuous man.

And the Hebrews missed it, too. Yahweh said, *"So I spoke to you; yet you would not listen (Deuteronomy 1:43).* You see, they decided that they would disregard what the Heavenly Father directed them to do and do what they thought was wise and prudent. That was their problem. They would not listen. Then Yahweh said, "You missed it. Take a little trip into the wilderness." Now, the Bible does not tell us how much time elapsed before the Hebrews repented, but I do not think it was long.

"'We have sinned against the Lord; we will go up and fight, just as the LORD our God commanded us.' And when everyone of you had girded on his weapons of war, you were ready to go into the mountain. And the Lord said to me, 'Tell them, "Do not go up nor fight, for I am not among you; . . . " **Then we turned and journeyed in the wilderness of the Way of the Red Sea, as the Lord spoke to me"** *(Deuteronomy 1:41 – 2:1)* were certain identifiable characteristics associated with the ministry of Yahshua two thousand years ago, there are a number of unchanging characteristics that can be observed about the gospel of Christ today. These characteristics clearly differentiate between the gospel of Yahshua and the gospel about him.

You see, they had missed Yahweh and His time. And His resolve was, You are not going in now. You are going to take a walk – forty years, and you are not coming back. You are not coming back. You lost it. You missed it. I am not with you. If you go in there now, you are going on your own. I am not with you. I am going to bless you. I know it is what I told you to do but I am not going with you now. I do not care if you have changed your mind, you are too late. You are headed to the wilderness. You will not go into the promised land.

Yahweh brought them out of Egypt with mighty signs and wonders. He brought them to the entrance into the promised land, the land that He had prepared for them to inherit. And they said, "Wait a minute. Wait until we can decide whether or not You know what You are talking about. We know You said, "Go," but we do not know if You looked that land over well or not." Now the God of the Hebrew fathers had already demonstrated His ability to deliver to provide for them. He already demonstrated His ability to deliver them from slavery. You would have thought that, based on that experience alone, that they could have believed Him for anything.

How critical Yahweh's timing is! Now, let me show you something. Moses spent forty years in the wilderness because he got ahead of Yahweh. The Hebrews, the people he was rescuing, spent forty years in the wilderness because they got behind Yahweh. He said, "You did not go into the promised land because you did not discern my time." Can you understand how important it is to discern the time of Yahweh in your life? Can you understand how important it is to wait on Him? You see, if you are waiting on Him, you will not rush off before you should, but when the moment comes you will be prepared.

Somehow, I believe that Yahweh made known to Moses that he was born and ordained to be a deliverer. At some point, Yahweh revealed his destiny to him. Having been adopted by Pharaoh's daughter, having been trained in the military of Egypt, having been educated in all of the academics of Egypt, he was a privileged man. Nevertheless, there was something in him that reached out, something in him that was offended by the oppression of his brothers, the Hebrews, were suffering. And he had the desire and the anointing to bring deliverance to these people. Certainly, in desiring to free his kinsmen, he was discerning the mind of the God of the Hebrews.

I am fully persuaded in my own heart that had Moses waited on Yahweh, he would have waited in Pharaoh's palace. Tell me where you would rather spend forty years. Would you rather spend forty years barely surviving or would you prefer to spend four decades living the lifestyle of the rich and famous? Come on, be honest; don't get religious. Where would you really rather be? Who said our Heavenly Father can only speak on the back side of the wilderness? Isaiah was not in the wilderness when Yahweh spoke to him. Daniel was not on the back side of the wilderness when he heard Yahweh. Ezra and Nehemiah were serving in the king's palace when they heard the voice of the Father. Who said Yahweh can only speak to you when everything has gone wrong? Who said He can only speak to you in the back side of the wilderness among smelly sheep? Who said that He can only speak through burning bushes? Where do believers ever get those ideas? They get them from religion.

I am persuaded that Yahweh did not change his timetables one day in order to accommodate Moses' failure. But I believe that for forty years Moses could have been in the Almighty's school even while living in Pharaoh's palace and could have avoided the wilderness altogether.

For out there, Moses got married. And by all evidence it was never a marriage planned in Heaven. Zipporah was of a different mind than Moses. In fact, she was so different by culture – her religion was so different, her understanding of the Creator was so different – that Moses allowed his sons to be raised without ever really confronting his wife about the need of circumcising them to keep covenant with his God. Forty years later, when they were headed back to Egypt, Yahweh confronted Moses about this issue. The Bible says Yahweh wanted to kill him. And the only way that Moses ever became willing to confront his wife about circumcising their sons was when the Creator of all that exists stood staring him in the face saying, "Son, if you take one more step, you are a dead man. Either you do what is required of a covenant Hebrew, or you are a dead man." Faced with the alternative, Zipporah was forced into obedience. But in anger and disgust, she took the foreskins she took the foreskins of her sons and threw them at Moses snarling, "You are a bloody husband." You see if Moses had waited on his God, no doubt Yahweh would have given him a Hebrew girl for a wife, not a pagan wife. That same wife was to cause trouble later on because Moses' family and the Hebrews never really accepted her.

You can pick up burdens. You can pick up liabilities out in the wilderness that you cannot shed when you come back. Some things you will be able leave in the wilderness. Some things you are going to be saddled with the rest of your life. Because you see, there are some relationships, some covenants you may enter into, that Yahweh will not allow you to break not even to do His will. While you are out in the wilderness, you may pick up some things that you must carry for the rest of your life. Oh, yes, the door of opportunity may still open to you and Yahweh will still be right on time. But how much easier it would be, how much better it would be to be unencumbered with those relationships and those things that are picked up in the wilderness. Had Moses waited on the God of the fathers, he could have continued to live where he was living. He did not have to endure all of suffering he experienced. He could have waited, and Yahweh would have taught him by His word and by His Spirit – just the way He wants to teach me and you.

When people preach about Moses, they will usually preach about burning bushes and voices of God and that is all wonderful. But there are some other things that took place out in the wilderness that were not so pleasant. Think about some of the things that went wrong for Moses out in the wilderness. First of all, he was separated from everybody he knew. It was a lonely place, and he, no doubt, was incredibly lonely much of the time. Then, he got married to a woman who was a constant problem for him the rest of his life.

Nevertheless, Moses, one of the great leaders of the Hebrew people spent about one third of his life in the wilderness because he got ahead of Yahweh. Only when he repented and turned aside to hear the Father's voice speaking to him was he led out of the wilderness. It was only then that he received the answers to some important questions. Who? When? Where? And how?

Yet not everyone who has gone into the wilderness has gone out of disobedience. Yahshua went into the wilderness out of obedience, not disobedience.

Immediately the Spirit drove Him into the wilderness. And He was there in the wilderness forty days, tempted by Satan, and was with the wild beasts; and the angels ministered to Him. (Mark 1:12-13, KJV)

Yahshua was driven by the Holy Spirit into the wilderness, not the desert, but into the wilderness. He found no strength there, but the ministering angels came to Him, ministered to Him, and strengthened Him in His ability to fulfill the purpose the Father had for Him in the wilderness. Yahshua did not choose to vacation in the wilderness. No, he was driven by the Holy Spirit. He was lured into the wilderness. He was not tempted into the wilderness. He was driven into the wilderness by the Holy Spirit indicating to me that there was a reluctance on His part to go into the wilderness. He did not choose to go there. It was not natural for Him to go there. Nor was it something He wanted to do.

I believe what Yahshua was experiencing in the wilderness was essentially what He was experiencing the night He was wrestling in Gethsemane. Yahshua did not *want* to go into Gethsemane. He did not want to go to the cross. He did not *want* to die on the cross. If you think he went hop, skippity, jump down to Gethsemane and was looking with keen, joyful anticipation to being nailed to the cross then you have missed revelation altogether. Yahshua was reluctant in His body and soul to go into Gethsemane. He wanted comfort. He wanted strength, and he was trying first of all to draw strength, to draw comfort, and to draw encouragement from those who were with Him in the flesh, but they by and large failed Him that night. Then Yahshua was supernaturally ministered to by angels who came there that evening with the express purpose of ministering to His all too human needs.

There is only one reason that Yahshua went to Gethsemane – because that was the Father's will. There was only one reason He went to the cross – to fulfill the will of the Father. And there was only one reason that Yahshua went into the wilderness and that also was to fulfill the will of the Father.

Here is an important truth. Everything that Yahshua did in going into the garden was for me. He did not go because there was some need in His life. He did not go because there was something that needed to be fulfilled in Him. He went into the Garden of Gethsemane for the purpose of accomplishing the Father's will and he went in there on my behalf. There was nothing that made Yahshua want to go to the cross. He went to the cross because it was the Father's will and He went to the cross for me and you. So, His reason for going into the garden was to fulfill the Father's will and to go there so that I do not have to go there. I know that you are glad today that the Messiah went to the cross. Why are you glad that Yahshua went to the cross? So that you do not have to go. Are you glad that Yahshua went to Hell? You know why he went to Hell? So, you do not have to go. Now, the same truth applies to His going into the wilderness. He went into the wilderness so that you do not have to go into the wilderness. If you believe and understand and accept that Yahshua went to the cross so that you do not have to then you do not run out every day and say, "Oh, Yahweh, just nail me to the cross." That is foolish! I do not want to go to the cross. What I do want is to be identified, by the Holy Spirit, with the Savior who did go to that cross and went to that cross in my place, on my behalf. Certainly, there is no need in both of us suffering.

Yahshua went into the wilderness, driven by the Spirit. It was not a vacation. It was not something He desired. He went there because it was His Father's will. He found no strength in the wilderness, but supernaturally imparted strength ministered to Him by the angels. It was not rest and recreation for Yahshua. He was facing the very powers of darkness. Why? So that you do not have to go there. And how can you avoid going there? Yahshua said, "Pray that you enter not in temptation." Pray and you will not find yourself in the wilderness.

CHAPTER THREE

WARNINGS ABOUT THE WILDERNESS

Now I have not always known what I know presently, and I have spent some time in the wilderness like these men of old. But I have not enjoyed one minute of one day of my wilderness wanderings. And I have learned now that I do not have to go into the wilderness. So, I am doing what Yahshua said. I am praying that I enter not into temptation. But what comes next?

You wait. Wait on Yahweh. Wait on His word. Wait on His time. Wait on the person to whom you are to be joined. Wait on His response. Simply wait on Him. Do not run off the first time Yahshua speaks. Wait on Him *"Wait on the Lord,"* Psalms 27:14 says, "[and] *be of good courage."* Wait on Yahweh. Wait on Yahweh.

There is a strong temptation whenever the Father reveals something to Believers, whenever He lays a job, a responsibility, a mission on your heart, to believe that it must be done now. And probably nowhere and in no way do we miss Yahweh more frequently than by rushing on with what we know in our hearts we have been called to do. And every time we rush ahead, we run straight into the wilderness. Not because we decided to disobey Yahweh. Not because we said, "I do not want to do what You want me to do." We get in the wilderness most of the time because we do not wait on Yahweh.

Most Christians do not rise up in rebellion against the will of Yahweh. They do not get into trouble because of disobedience. Some of the worst experiences I have had as a Believer have come because I knew the overall call of the Father, but I did not wait on Him for specifics. For instance, in my case, I knew I was called to preach. I was called into the ministry. So, if you are called to preach, it must mean that you go preach. I mean, why would Yahweh call you to preach if you are not preaching? If He called you to preach and you are not preaching, you must be out of His will, right? Well, that is the natural way of thinking about it. What is the natural response? Doors open. People call you. They recommend you. "Oh, I think there is a good opportunity down here. Now, this little place is not very much, but…" And there is pressure. I guarantee you that every person who has been called into the ministry for any length of time has already had invitations to get started. And none of them were from Yahweh. They were from family, friends, and denominational leaders.

As far as I know, I have never openly disobeyed Yahweh. Not one time when He has dealt with me about His will have I drawn back from Him. I have never said, "Yahweh, I do not want to do that."

But I have been in some wilderness experiences as a Believer, and every time I got in the wilderness, I go there because I did not wait on Him. I knew He had called me. I knew He had called me to preach. I knew He had put this desire to preach in my Spirit and I wanted to let it out. I wanted to do what He had called me to do. After all, that is what I had been taught was being faithful. That is what I had been taught was being obedient to the Heavenly Father – to do what He had called you to do.

Sadly, I pastored some churches while I was in the wilderness and those congregations were in the wilderness, too. I have had some horrible experiences pastoring. And yet, there has never been a question in my heart that Yahweh called me to preach that He called me to oversee.

I feel so sorry for many pastors today because they do not have a word from Yahweh. They have a call of Yahweh, but it is a general call. They know only that they are called into the ministry. And they miss Yahweh's timing out of a sense of urgency to be faithful. Receiving the call into the ministry is merely a first step. That is about all that is. What do you need to know in order to be faithful to your call? You need to know not only that what, but also you need to know *when, who, how, and where.*

Take a look at the Levites. A Levite was a Levite from the day of his birth. Paul, Jeremiah, and others talk about being called of Yahweh before they were ever born. I believe I was called into ministry before I was born even though it took me a long time to arrive at a conscious revelation of the call on my life. Paul recognized that even during all the years he was ranting and raving and trying to kill Christians that Yahweh had set him apart to be what he became - a chief apostle and one to take the kingdom message to the Gentiles. You see, the purpose, the plan of Yahweh was established long before you and I ever came along. In the life of a Levite, he was recognized as a Levite in training when he became twenty years old. And for ten years all he did was carry water, cut firewood, and clean up after the altar priests. He spent ten years in apprenticeship. When he was thirty years old, he was ready to begin his official duties.

Yet the modern Church sends twenty-year-old preachers out that do not have anything together. They do not have their family life together. They do not have their finances together. They have nothing but the call of Yahweh so most of them are sent out into the wilderness. And the sad testimony is that is where most of them perish. They go out and get locked into a system and they perish in the wilderness.

One of the most difficult things a pastor has to do sometimes is restrain a young man called of Yahweh. Oh, he has got to go. The whole world is dying. Well, it was dying when he got here and it will be dying after he is gone. How presumptuous it is to think that the world's salvation depends upon one man. Come on! Give Yahweh more credit than that. He is not going to cast all of His eggs into one basket.

I could have saved myself a lot of trouble if I had received this revelation years ago. I tried to preach having never done so before. The first pastor's office I was ever in was my own, yet I tried to pastor when I had never been pastored.

One man I know said he started pastoring when he was fifteen years old. Years later, he said, "Don't you know a lot of wisdom was coming out of that pulpit!"

So, you need to know *what, when, where, and how*. Finally, Moses realized he needed to know who because he could not accomplish his purpose by himself. He needed his brother. Let me tell you that no matter what Yahweh has called you to be in this life, there is somebody to help you fulfill your call. You say, "Well, Yahweh has called me to do …." Well, who is to assist you? There is somebody in your life who is to help you fulfill your call. Pastors, never was that a more timely word. Yahweh did not call me or you to be a lone ranger. Yahweh did not call us to submerge ourselves into an organization. He called us to be joined. I tell you that every man Yahweh really uses is going to be joined to somebody – not to a system, not to a doctrine, but to somebody.

And once you discover who is joined to you, wait until you know when you are to act. Quit rushing. Quit trying to manipulate. Some people think, "I have got to get married. I have got to get married." You are going to get married, but it will not be Yahweh's man or Yahweh's woman because the Devil hears and rushes somebody into place and says, "Ah, I have got an important job for you. Let me dress you up. Let me give you all the right words." So he rushes the counterfeit out and you respond, "Oh, Yahweh has answered my prayers!"

Know this. If the answer came in thirty minutes, it is not Yahweh. Yahweh does not get into a hurry. Remember James' encouragement, *Let patience have its perfect work that you may be perfect and complete, lacking nothing" (James 1:4 NKJV).* Do you believe Yahweh? "Oh, but, preacher, He said ...l" He said! Yeah! Did you see it worked out? Did you see it carried out? Did you observe a while? "Oh, I know everybody else is foolish, but I am wise. I know everybody else should wait a while, but I am ready to go. Everybody else needs time to mature, but I am ready now." You are headed for the wilderness, headed for the wilderness, headed for the wilderness.

One of the temptations Satan used against Yahshua was to urge him to get ahead of His Father's time. I believe that Satan often has better perception of our prophetic purpose than we do.

Moses could not do the will of Yahweh outside the proper time, without the proper relationships. All of these factors entered into him being prepared but he tried to rush along. He heard the voice of Yahweh; no question about that. But he did not wait. He did not pray. He did not let patience have its perfect work. He rushed in, made decisions, and wound up in the wilderness.

How much better to wait on the Lord! How much better to wait on His timing. When Yahweh puts together a puzzle, you do not have to make the pieces fit. Have you ever bought something and it was not quite right but you did not want to be bothered with going back and exchanging it, so you tried to make it fit? Ladies, have you ever had the experience of sewing a dress, and something was not quite right, but you continued sewing and you were never really happy with it? It never really satisfied you. For so much of our lives we are trying to make things fit. We are trying to push puzzle pieces together so that they resemble the picture we have of what life should be like. We are trying to force the puzzle pieces to work. I know this, that whenever the plan of Yahweh is followed, things will come together in a beautiful fashion. The servant of the living god must not strive. You do not have to make it happen. You do not have to persuade people for it to happen. The Heavenly Father will fit it together. He will make it work for you – if you will wait on Him. It may not make sense to you now, but there is a plan, there is a purpose, there is a divine will for every person born. If you will seek Yahweh, if you will pray diligently, Yahweh will put the puzzle together for you. He will form the picture of your life for you.

Sometimes we have to get over the embarrassment of saying, "I was wrong. I was premature. I got ahead of Yahweh." Some people arrive at their own marriage ceremony and suddenly realize that this joining is not right but because of all of the invitations, the showers, and the family expectations, they go through with something that their spirit testifies against. How much better to wait on the Lord! How much better to say, "I was wrong." How much better to say, "Let us wait a while, and have it God's way with His perfect peace and His joy."

You see, anything that you decide to do, if you do not have Yahweh's full approval, is presumptuous. Moses said of the Hebrews,

"You would not listen, but rebelled against the command of the Lord, and presumptuously went up into the mountain" (Deuteronomy 1:43, NKJV).

They reasoned, "I am going to do … I am going to say …. I am going to go…" No, if your action is not in perfect harmony with the divine purpose for your life, it is presumptuous of you to think that you can go anywhere or that you can do anything.

You see, when we talk about temptation, most of the time we think about something that is immoral, something that is terrible. But you can miss the purpose for your life over a good thing. Temptation is not always a temptation into what we call sin. Temptation is not always a temptation to do something immoral. Temptation is not always a desire to do something illegal. Temptation is not always a strong pull to do something that is contrary to righteousness. Most believers do not get into trouble because they enter into the temptation to be immoral, or to commit illegal acts, or to behave contrary to the will of their Heavenly Father. Yet, they end up in the wilderness because somewhere along the road they missed the purpose of Yahweh for their lives.

Nor do you need burning bushes in your life to learn the will of Yahweh. What you need is the word of Yahweh and the Spirit of Yahweh. Sooner or later, if you learn anything about the Creator, you are going to learn it through His word and His Spirit. You say, "Well,

I just believe in experience." Explain to me, then, why two people can have the same experience and one person comes out praising Yahweh, and the other one comes out bitter. If experience teaches anything then why do they not both have the same response? Because experience is not what teaches. It reveals. It exposes but it does not teach.

What teaches, what changes a person is when he gets hold of Yahweh's word and allows the Holy Spirit to work that word until it becomes faith in his heart. The experience will simply reveal to what extent the person has received the grace of Yahweh. It will simply reveal to what extent he has believed the word of Yahweh and allowed the Holy Spirit to work in him. You see, the experienced – the testing – does not teach anything. It simply pulls back the cover. It reveals the truth of what a person is. For example, if you go through hard times and in those hard times you praise Yahweh, the experience did not cause you to praise Yahweh. You learned as a matter of faith by hearing the word of Yahweh and responding to the Spirit a long time ago – before you ever got into the heartbreaking experience. You learned something about praising Yahweh, so that when the experience came, you were prepared. The experience did not teach you. It just revealed what you had already learned by the word and the Spirit. Another man may get into that same experience and he may not have prayed. He may not have received the Word of Yahweh. He may not be walking in the Spirit. So, when he gets into that same situation, he responds, "I do not know why Yahweh hates me! I do not know why Yahweh took me! I do not know!" The reason this man acts the way he does is not because of the bad experience but because he never prayed. He never set himself to seek first the kingdom of Yahweh. He never set the word of Yahweh before him.

Yahweh has profound ways of summing things up. In the Old Testament, He summarizes His kingdom in *Deuteronomy 28*. Moses relayed Yahweh's instructions to the Hebrews,

Now it shall come to pass, if you diligently obey the voice of the Lord your God, to observe carefully all His commandments which I command you today, that the Lord your God will set you high above all nations of the earth. ***And all these blessings shall come upon you and overtake you, because you obey the voice of the Lord your God.*** *(Deuteronomy 28:1-2, NKJV)*

In Matthew 6:33, Yahshua summarized more concisely than Moses, *"But seek the kingdom of God and His righteousness, and all these things shall be added to you."* What Moses and Yahshua were saying to their people was – seek the kingdom of Yahweh by setting the word of Yahweh before you and determine to both hear and do whatever He says. Do not turn to the right. Do not turn to the left. Set your face like a flint to see, to know, and to do the word of Yahweh, both the word in recorded Scripture and whatever word the Holy Spirit puts into your heart because that is the *will of Yahweh.*

I am living today, not only by the word in the book, the Bible, but I am living by the word that the Spirit of Yahweh has put into my heart. Most of what I am experiencing today does not come out of that book. It comes out of me praying and seeking Yahweh.

When you are in leadership there is always a lot of pressure to move at the advice of other people. And if you go by that, you are going to wind up spending your life in the wilderness. Even if you go to other counselors (and maybe in the course of carrying out your responsibilities you have to do that), do not make a decision sitting around the conference table. Do not make a decision until you have laid the issue before Yahweh and before those whom Yahweh has put in your life.

A man who has come to me for some counseling complimented me by saying, "You know everything you have said to me has been right." My response was, "Let me tell you something. Do not get the idea that Nolan Ball is smart. I believe I could have told you the most foolish thing in the world, and it would be wisdom because first of all I have set myself under the headship of Yahshua the Anointed One. And, in turn, you have set yourself under me and recognized that Yahweh put me in your life. Together we have been obedient."

What is that obedience? It is hearing and doing the word of Yahweh. That is the reason that my counsel becomes wisdom.

And wisdom is vital to those who find themselves in the wilderness because the wilderness is a dangerous place. It is a place outside of Yahweh's purpose, outside of His safety, **outside of His protection**. The dangers found in the wilderness are not only those that brought you to this place of disobedience. The wilderness itself holds certain inherent dangers. Once you are in the wilderness, you are exposed to even more temptations and dangers. Negatives begin to compound themselves. Problems begin to multiply. It is awfully easy to compromise your convictions in the wilderness, to compromise the truth of Yahweh. It is awfully easy to compromise the covenant of Yahweh's relationship when you walk in the wilderness.

And it is easy to get lost, really lost, in the wilderness. There are no warning signs, no signs providing directions in the desolate places. An incident forever seared in my mind from my early adolescence illustrates this point very well. I came home from school one day when I was twelve or thirteen and decided to go squirrel hunting. I grabbed my rifle and went down into the river swamp where I knew there were plenty of squirrels. And I was a good hunter that day because I killed a few of them. Now when it got near dusk, I knew I needed to get out of the swamp and go home. On my way out of the swamp, I heard another squirrel barking and I foolishly decided to see if I could kill him, too. So, I went down this little, logging road that had no outlet; it was a dead end. Suddenly, I was turned around. I lost my bearings. I was as lost as a man has ever been lost. Now, if I had stayed where I had been and gone home, I would have been all right. But I went down one road too many, and I got lost. Believers who find themselves in the wilderness are like I was – deceived into thinking there is something worth going after down the next path. You can get utterly lost running down this road and running down that path trying to find Yahweh. Yahweh is not in the wilderness. It is not the natural habitat for the Believer, either. It is not a safe place. All the roads in the wilderness are dead end roads.

Now, I wish I could tell you today that I had never been in the wilderness. I wish I could tell you that, but I cannot. However, what I am declaring to you today is that by divine grace, I do not ever intend to go there again. I do not like the wilderness, and neither should you.

F. Nolan Ball

CHAPTER FOUR
HOW TO RESPOND IN THE WILDERNESS

What should a Believer do when he finds himself lost deep in the wilderness, and all the roads are dead-end roads? If you are in a place that is terrible and suddenly you look into your heart and realize you are there not because of obedience – you are, in fact, there because of disobedience – what is the proper response? Repent. Repent quickly! Do not rejoice if you are out in the wilderness. Do not rejoice if you look into your heart and it rises up and says *You are not here because of obedience; you are here because of disobedience.* A smart person would say,

"Uh-oh, I missed a turn in the road. I am out here in a difficult place. Things are not going well, and I know I am here because of disobedience. So, I am not going to play a religious game; I am not going to join the crowd down in the charismatic meeting and praise and worship the Lord as though there is nothing wrong. No, I am going to deal with my problem. I am going to repent of my disobedience."

The smart person does not start multiplying the problem by making more mistakes. He just sits down, gets control of himself, and says, "Wait just a minute. Why am I here? Where did I miss it?"

Let me say again, for most of us, it is not going to be rebellion that we need to repent of. For most of us, it is not going to be some immoral act that we need to repent from. For most of us it is not going to be some illegal thing that we have done. Most people will need to repent of impetuousness, not immorality. No, you do not have to look into your heart and find rebellion to know that you are in the wilderness. You only have to look and realize that you missed Yahweh's turnoff. You missed His time. Then you will need to repent for getting ahead of Yahweh, of running off before He completely revealed His plan. We human beings are always in a hurry. But our Heavenly Father is looking for somebody who understands that He is eternal. He does not have to complete a task before sundown. He does not have to accomplish this week all He is ever going to do.

But does the person in the wilderness need to do anything besides repent? Yes, there are several commonsense steps to take after you have repented. The repentant wanderer would be wise to follow these steps if he intends to walk out of the wilderness one day.

Number one: Come to grips with the awful fact that some things are lost forever. When you miss Yahweh's timing, you cannot go back. Now that is difficult to accept. Because Yahweh is so big and so smart and so superlative in all that He does and is, we believe that, somehow, He will take our situation and make it brand new again. Certainly, He could do that, but in His wisdom, he rarely does. The Hebrews eventually went into the promised land, but all of the people who initially refused to go in, were never allowed entrance. That day was over, that day was finished, that opportunity was gone. It is so important that you wait on Yahweh and respond at the right time.

Desert or Wilderness

Over the years I have seen friends miss Yahweh's time. And from that point, things began to go wrong in their lives even though their wilderness wanderings did not develop out of rebellion against the Father. I have witnessed a lot of divorces and a tremendous number of extremely serious problems occur – not out of rebellion but out of missing Yahweh's timing. Recently, I have stood in some places and mused to myself about what might have been, if certain people had not missed Yahweh's timing, but I will never know what might have been because those days can never be recaptured.

Nor can a person go back and be a child once again. So many times, people spend fruitless years of their lives trying to create what never was, trying to grasp hold of something that never was, and truthfully can never be. Some people were robbed of a decent childhood, and when they come to Yahshua, they want to go back and recreate what never was. It will not help you at all to be dreaming about the might-have beens, living with missed opportunities and things you are not in control of. So, be prepared to recognize and acknowledge that some things cannot be recaptured. If you are struggling with relationships that bother you because they never were right, come to grips with the fact that some relationships are lost. Some things can never be retrieved. Some paths can never be walked again. But Yahweh's grace is big enough to cover it all. His mercy, His healing power is big enough, great enough, powerful enough, all-encompassing enough to make it right for you.

And if you will let Him, He will heal you. Yahweh is not going to take you back and let you live your childhood over again with an earthly father. But if He were not a healer of hurts and wounds, and empty places, there would be no real peace and joy. But I am declaring to you today that my Heavenly Father is a healer. Yahweh is a healer. No matter what kind of hurts, no matter what kind of wounds, no matter what kind of empty places there are in your life, Yahweh will not simply make it better. He will heal your pain. He will deliver you from emotional scars.

Leave it with Yahweh. He is gracious and full of compassion and mercy, and He forgives all that we repent of. He is a healer. If some of you had made the right decisions, if you had waited on Yahweh, you would not have ended up in divorce. But the worst thing you can do is to berate yourself for the rest of your life. Yahweh is a healer. He is a forgiver. There is no need in saying, "Well, look at what would have happened if I…" Look, we could all fill our days with "If I…" or "What if?…" and "Well, if I had only…" But you did not do it, and I did not do it. That door is closed. That opportunity is gone.

You may be one wanting to get out of the wilderness, but you keep wanting to pull everything that you have experienced with you. You want to take a piece of heavy luggage with you. In this piece of luggage are hurts and relationships. And you want to take these things with you and keep trying to make them right. But this luggage is such a heavy thing that you really cannot get where you are supposed to be going because you keep pulling this heavy luggage with you. You must release it. Put the bondage behind you. Just release the luggage and the baggage and walk out of the wilderness into what Yahweh has for you. Do not let those things bog you down and prevent you from walking toward the fullness of what He has for you. Leave them there and let Him heal you from those things. Do not keep trying to drag the past with you everywhere you go.

I pray Yahweh will help you not to spend one day beating up yourself about missed opportunities. Every one of us has wished at times that our foot could turn around so we could kick ourselves right where it would do some good. But we were not created with that kind of anatomy. So, do not spend your life consumed with what might have been. It is not. It is never going to be. Settle it. Accept it. Yahweh is gracious. Every day is a new beginning. Every day is a new opportunity. Do not waste today by regretting yesterday. Today is the day that we have to live. Today we can do something about the will of the Father. Today He is talking. Today He is giving direction. You do not have to live the rest of your life regretting and bemoaning what never was or never can be. There is a way out of the wilderness. Yahweh has a plan. He has a purpose for your life. I am encouraged by the knowledge that He has a plan and purpose for my life, and He has one for yours as well. And you can find it, and you can know it, and you can live it out. All has not been lost.

So, forget about the past that is lost to you and take the next step in walking out of the wilderness. Prepare the next generation to inherit the promise.

The Hebrews had to come to grips with the fact that one generation was not going into the promised land. That particular generation of people would not go in, then could not go in, and in fact, did not go in. Now, it would have been a horrible thing if they had just spent the next forty years, bewailing and bemoaning that they missed it. The strange thing is that though they missed it, Yahweh gave to them a tremendous responsibility. That responsibility was to train the next generation—to train their children. Sometimes if we are not careful, we will become so disillusioned, so embittered, so angry toward the Father, and so angry toward ourselves and others that we throw away our children's opportunities.

You see, there was no guarantee that the next generation was going in. I believe with all of my heart that the reason the second generation went in was that their parents learned their lesson. The original participants of the exodus settled the fact that they were not going to inherit the promised land. They stopped weeping, wailing, and gnashing their teeth about what could not be.

What can we do when we end up in the wilderness? We can learn from the original wanderers. We can teach our children to know the Father's voice. We can teach our children to wait on Him. We can teach our children so that when the door is open again, Yahweh can take them in.

The tragedy of poverty is not just that individuals are caught in it, but so often it destroys the ability of the parents to do anything about elevating their children out of it. So, poverty and its accompanying hopelessness are perpetuated from generation to generation.

But Yahweh is wanting to raise up a generation today that will say, "Thank You for where we came from. Thank You that there is more ground to be gained. There is more to be experienced. Now I am going to let my children stand on my shoulders, I am going to lift them up a little higher. I will talk honestly about my failures, but I am not going to bemoan my shortcomings. I am not going to be controlled by them. I am going to try to help my children and my grandchildren, learn from my mistakes, learn from my successes, and stand on my shoulders and see a little farther, and go a little farther, and do a little more."

In order to do that, I must do away with anger toward my Heavenly Father. I must do away with bitterness toward myself. I must get over blaming everybody else and take authority over where I am and the people that He has given me to train and nurture for the coming generation. There was a generation that went in. It was not the first one, but the second generation went in and possessed the land.

Many times in a military invasion, the first wave may not make it. But their buddies coming behind them will walk over their dead bodies and take a beachhead and establish the presence of the invading army, because somebody laid down their lives. Life does not have to be that way, but that is the way that it often happens.

How foolish it would be for us to spend our days bemoaning what was not and what cannot ever be. Let us take opportunity. Let us seize the opportunity and do something with it prepare another generation to go a little farther.

In order to do that, you may have to adjust your eschatology. You are never going to be training another generation if all you are thinking about is escaping from the earth in the rapture that must surely be imminent. If you are possessed with the idea that the Savior may come today, you are never going to prepare yourself for tomorrow, and you are not going to prepare anybody else for tomorrow. That has been one of the plagues of the Pentecostal movement over the last half century – that we were so encumbered to this idea that Yahshua the Messiah may come today, that we never really prepared a generation to take a nation, to take a world for Him. We never prepared a generation to go in and seize the promised land and see the kingdom of Yahweh established.

We may be the first wave of troops. We may be left on the shore – nothing but dead men for others to step on and step over, but somebody is going to establish the kingdom of Yahweh in the earth. And I believe that we can make sure that this generation and the coming generation goes in and does what Yahshua said to do – make disciples of all nations, preach the gospel in all the world, and bear witness of Yahshua the Messiah. So, prepare the second generation.

Then, expect Yahweh to reveal Himself. Some of the greatest revelations to men from the Creator came during wilderness experiences. Now, I would rather not go into the wilderness, even if there are burning bushes and shaking mountains out there. But if you end up in the wilderness, let me encourage you with this: The Father does not forsake you. If you repent, He rushes to come to you. And He will provide for you. He will provide water out of the rock. Whatever you need, He will provide. If it is manna from heaven, He will provide it. If it is fiery communication, He will provide it. Whatever it is, your Father in Heaven will provide it. So, expect that even in the wilderness, even when you have missed His will and His purpose, He will show up and will manifest Himself in His miraculous ways to you in order to call you back to His purpose.

Remember this – Yahweh does not forsake His own. He will never leave you, even if you miss a turn in the road. He will never leave you, even if you miss an opportunity. He will never leave you. "My commitment," He would say, "is to you. It is not to your obedience; it is not to your success. My commitment is to you. And I will never leave you." People will leave you. People will call you false. People will forsake you. People will not want to be identified with you, your failures, and your wilderness wanderings, but your Heavenly Father is never ashamed of you. He will never forsake you. He will always be there. He is always ready to restore you.

I think it strange, but I also think it true, that Yahweh seems to choose to do His greatest miracles for those who missed the road. Those who are walking in wisdom and understanding and those walking in His timetable seem to never see anything or hear anything spectacular. Maybe it is because they do not need it. Maybe He saves the spectacular. Maybe He reserves the great miracle for those who have missed it, to say to them in a spectacular way, "I know you. I know where you are. You are not where you are supposed to be, but I still know where you are. And I know what you are going through. And I have not forsaken you."

So be prepared to turn aside and listen when He speaks. Do not make the same mistake you made before. Yahweh will talk to you. He does not become sullen, like we sometimes do at each other. He does not pout. He keeps communicating. He keeps talking. So, you need to position yourself, train yourself, to listen to the Father's voice, because you will never get out of the wilderness if you do not hear Him.

One day there came a time when the God of the Hebrew fathers said, "Okay. Enough is enough is enough. It is time to go. It is time to turn north. You have been around this mountain enough times; head toward the land I promised you." If you are in the wilderness today, and you feel like your years have spent going around and around and around in circles, the God of Abraham, Isaac, and Jacob wants to talk to you. He has a word for you about how to get out of your circumstance, how to get out of the wilderness.

You, therefore, need to develop the ability to listen. Listen to the Ancient of Days. Listen to His Holy Spirit in the earth today. Husbands, listen to your wives. Wives, listen to your husbands. Children, listen to your parents. Listen to the apostle in your life. Listen to the prophet in your life. Listen to your pastor. Now that does not mean you have to be controlled by anybody but listen to them. Listen to the people Yahweh has placed in your life. He may be speaking to you through them. Hear what they have to say. Do not compound the problem – listen.

Finally, set yourself–this time to obey. Set yourself to not be moved by people or circumstance or anything. But when your Father speaks, be ready to go, be ready to move.

When He does speak, respond. That is how you are going to get out of the wilderness – by turning aside, listening, and obeying whenever He speaks.

Do you want to get out of your wilderness experience? Then repent, recognize, and come to grips with the fact that some things are lost and cannot be recovered. Do not give up. Begin to prepare yourself and to prepare those coming behind you. Prepare the next generation. Expect the Heavenly Father to reveal Himself to you and turn aside and listen when He speaks. Then set yourself to do all that He says. And you will walk out of the wilderness because Yahweh will show you the only path that is available to you. It is a narrow path, but it will lead you out of the wilderness. And it will probably lead you directly into Yahweh's desert.

CHAPTER FIVE
DESERT DWELLERS

Remember the desert is Yahweh's preparation place for His people. It is where He prepares them for what is to come next. It is a good place, a safe place. It is a place of rest, a place of peace.

When you are in the will of Yahweh, in His desert, you are in His preparation place. Now, one of the ways you can know that you are in the Father's preparation place is when you look deep within yourself there is divine peace. You may not be able to explain it; you may not be able to persuade anyone else to believe that you really are doing quite fine. They may say, "Well, I am just going to pray for you anyway. I know you are putting on a front; I know you are just making a positive confession. I know it cannot really be that good, so I am going to pray for you."

But it really is that good. It really is that good, because when you are in Yahweh's desert places, your life is not being judged or controlled by externals. It is being controlled by what you know within.

Let me explore this concept of the desert being Yahweh's preparation place with you looking at four people in the Scriptures, two out of the Old Covenant and two out of the New Covenant.

First of all, I want to look at Joseph, Joseph the dreamer. Joseph was the youngest of twelve sons born to Jacob. As a young fellow he had a dream and in his dream he understood that his father and his mother and all of his brothers were going to bow down to him and that he was going to rule over them. Yet, when he told his family his dream they did not like it.

His older brothers did not like him in the first place because he was Daddy's favorite. So, when he recounted his dream, his brothers wanted to kill him. However, one brother convinced the others to sell him into slavery instead. He was taken to Egypt and became a slave of Potiphar, the captain of Pharaoh's guard.

For a time, life was very good for Joseph. He proved to be a faithful and trusted steward over all of Potiphar's household. In time, Potiphar's wife became so enamored and attracted to this young man with his winning ways that she connived to lure Joseph into adultery. In a fit of rage, because Joseph scorned her sexual advances, Potiphar's wife accused him of attempting to rape her.

He was thrown in prison where he interpreted the dreams of Pharaoh's chief butler and baker. But when the butler was released from prison, he conveniently forgot the aid and comfort Joseph had given him when he was incarcerated. He did not speak to Pharaoh on Joseph's behalf until two years later when Pharaoh had a dream, none of his magicians could interpret. Only then did the chief butler remember the man in the prison who could interpret dreams.

So, it came to pass that when Joseph was thirty years old, he interpreted Pharaoh's dream and was made second in command in all of Egypt. Then when famine struck the land, and his brothers – the same brothers who sold him into slavery – came begging to buy food, he received them and provided for their needs. And Jacob and all of Joseph's family came to Egypt and bowed down to him.

Follow the trail of Joseph. No matter where he is, no matter what he is doing, Joseph never accepted the mentality of a slave. And you know what happened? He was always in charge. Even when he was a slave, he was in charge. Because you see, this dream of being a leader would not allow him to become a slave. This dream of being a man anointed of Yahweh and prepared of Yahweh to be a leader would not allow him ever to accept for one day the mentality of a slave.

So, it did not matter whether he was in a man's house who owned him like a piece of chattel. Even in refusing to violate the trust placed in him by Potiphar, Joseph remained true to the call of Yahweh upon his life and fled from the woman.

Centuries later Apostle Paul would warn another young man that sometimes the better way to deal with lust is to run. He did not act like a slave, and Potiphar did not treat him like a slave. Potiphar made him a steward over everything he had. Even when he went to jail, he did not accept the mentality of a slave and the prison keeper made him a ruler in the jail.

You see, this young man had a dream in his heart that nothing could take away from him, so every time somebody tried to send him into the wilderness, he just turned it into Yahweh's desert. He concluded; *Yahweh is using this to prepare me for the realization of my dream.*

You must learn to live like that. You must have a word from Yahweh. You have got to believe. You have got to know that no matter where you are today, you are in Yahweh's time. You are on His schedule. You are on His track. You have not jumped track. You have not gone down a dead-end street. You have not missed it. You are not behind. You are right on time.

I live in the confidence that the steps of a righteous person are directed and ordered. They are timed of Yahweh. I live in that confidence. I live with that dream in my heart. I tell you I am going to become what Yahweh called me to become. I am going to do what He called me to do because I am believing the word that I have in my heart. Many times if I had believed circumstances I could have said, "Uh-oh, I missed it. I missed it." But I refused to believe I missed it. I believe even my misses are hits.

Yahweh does not always look at my actions. He looks at the attitude of my heart. He looks at the faith of my heart. He looks at me believing. He sees me refusing to accept some things. Joseph had to refuse the mentality of a slave. He had to refuse bitterness. In fact, he named his first son *I will not remember* (Manasseh). Every time he talked to his son, every time he called his name, he was saying, I am not going to be bitter at anybody. I am not going to hold a grudge against my brothers. I am not going to hold a grudge against Potiphar's wife. I am not going to hold a grudge against the chief butler who forgot me. I am looking to Yahweh.

If people reject you, do not worry about it. There is somebody out there that Yahweh has purposed for you to be joined to. There is somebody who will come into your life. You know Joseph probably looked at the baker and the butler and thought, *Oh, maybe one of these boys is the one who will deliver me.* Although it may not be the person you think it will be, Yahweh has somebody with whom you are to be joined. He has a time. He has a way. But you cannot ever accept the mentality of a slave.

Can you imagine what it is like to hold a high position then be publicly humiliated and shamed by being unjustly accused of trying to rape a woman, who was herself doing the propositioning, and then being thrown into prison where you are forgotten? Then you help someone who had a similar position to yours, and he gets out of prison but does nothing to help you get out?

Can I tell you that you will always have to face up to rejection? I do not believe you can fulfill the dreams and the visions that Yahweh births in your heart without accusations. And if you do not know that you have the word of Yahweh, you will get off course. You will get off track. You will begin to fight back and you will begin to retaliate. You will begin to receive accusations.

But Joseph received neither accusations, bitterness, nor rejection. He was not languishing in prison. He was serving Yahweh there. He was being faithful. He was dreaming dreams and staying true to the confession of his word. And one day, the keeper of the prison said, "Joseph, Pharaoh wants you. Pharaoh needs help. He has heard that you know how to understand and interpret dreams and visions." And Joseph did, because he had practiced interpreting dreams and visions. He was able to interpret other people's dreams and visions because he learned to interpret and visualize the dreams and visions of his own heart.

So, Joseph became a desert dweller. He learned how to allow the Father to prepare his purpose in life by keeping him hidden away. And he did not learn how to just survive in the desert. He learned how to thrive there.

Now David was another faithful Old Testament believer. He, too, learned some things out in the desert. He could have been out there cursing sheep all day long.

Stinking sheep. Stinking sheep. Stinking sheep. Dumb sheep. Dumb sheep. Dumb sheep. I pulled that lamb out of the last hole. If he gets into another hole, I am not pulling him out ever again.

But David used his desert experiences to learn how to praise and worship the Creator, to become the sweet psalmist of Israel. He did not develop that gift at a conservatory of music. David did not develop his gifts of music and singing because he was planning a career as a worship leader, playing and singing, worshipping Yahweh was his means of survival. Anyone can sing when the sun is shining bright but you need a song in your heart at night. He learned out in the desert where Yahweh had placed him. He learned how to begin walking in his purpose out there where it would have been easy to be bitter and resentful of the fact that his brothers were off doing the important tasks, big stuff, the stuff that big boys do, while he was out there watching over the sheep.

But instead of wasting his time and profiting from his desert experiences, David learned how to defeat the devourers. He learned how to fight. He learned how to war spiritually. He learned how to defeat the devourers of loneliness, depression, and rejection with music, with praise. When the time came for him to soothe Saul from his tormenting spirits, he knew how because he had been practicing. When he had been lonely in the desert, he had encouraged himself with music. When he became depressed and felt as if his father and his brothers were rejecting him, he encouraged himself by playing and singing psalms of praise, psalms of rejoicing. He chose to become a worshipper instead of a grumbler, to become a singer, to become a musician, to become one who praised the God of Israel. As David took that attitude to work with him every day, everything he saw became a testimony to the goodness of Yahweh. He did not just see hills. He saw hills standing up and praising Yahweh. He did not see trees. He saw trees clapping their hands. He did not just see rain. He felt Yahweh in the rain. He could do that because of the dreams and the vision that Yahweh was putting in his heart as a young man.

He also learned how to war naturally out in the desert. He learned how to sling a stone with a slingshot to protect the sheep from wild animals. Sometimes he engaged in bare handed combat with these mighty beasts. In this way he had killed the fiercest animals in the land: lions and bears. He had come face to face with his enemies in the desert and learned to destroy them. He learned to allow a fierce, protective anger to energize him in order to deny the enemy anything in his care.

And while in the desert, David learned how to believe Yahweh. He learned to trust Him. He learned how to hear His voice. He came to know the Creator as perhaps no other person.

David profited from his desert experience. When he was called out of the desert and anointed to be king, he was fully equipped to fulfill his purpose. He had been protected from becoming carnally minded. While David was in the desert, his brothers had been fighting battles, but when they saw Goliath, they concluded *No one can defeat this Philistine.* But when David saw him and heard him defy Saul's army, the army of the Living God, he did not judge with a carnal mind. He saw by faith that this enemy was not only challenging Saul's army, he was issuing an open challenge and deriding the power of the Almighty. David saw with spiritual eyes and judged that this Philistine was no different from the lion or the bear that had come to devour his earthly father's sheep. This beast was attempting to devour his Heavenly Father's army.

Long ago David had chosen to be faithful to defend what belonged to his earthly father; he decided to be faithful over what had been given to another man. Now, David determined that he would defend what belonged to his Heavenly Father. He would not cower in the face of the devourer. He would do what he had always done. He would challenge and defeat the enemy that sought to destroy what had been placed in his hands.

Since David had already been anointed king, the army was, in reality, his, not Saul's – but more importantly to David, it was Yahweh's army. First Samuel tells us that David came against the giant as he had with the lion and the bear, and he defeated the enemy of Israel. When did David attain this valor? Where did he learn to use a slingshot? In the desert, of course.

The first New Covenant desert dweller we encounter in the Scriptures is John, who became known as John the Baptist, but perhaps a more appropriate title would have been John the Prophet.

Now Elizabeth's full time came for her to be delivered, and she brought forth a son. When her neighbors and relatives heard how the Lord had shown great mercy to her, they rejoiced with her. Now so it was, on the eighth day, that they came to circumcise the child; and they would have called him by the name of his father, Zacharias. And his mother answered and said, "No; he shall be called John." But they said to her, "There is no one among your relatives who is called by this name." So, they made signs to his father – what he would have him called. And he asked for a writing tablet, and wrote, saying, "His name is John." And they all marveled. Immediately his mouth was opened and his tongue loosed, and she spoke praising God. Then fear came on all those who dwelt around them; and all these sayings were discussed throughout all the hill country of Judea. And all those who heard them kept them in their hearts, saying, "What kind of child will this be?" And the hand of the Lord was with him. Now his father Zacharias was filled with the Holy Spirit, and prophesied, saying, Blessed is the Lord God of Israel, for He has visited and redeemed His people, and has raised up a horn of salvation for us in the house of His servant David, as He spoke by the mouth of His holy prophets, who have been since the world began, that we should be saved from our enemies and from the hand of all who hate us, to perform the mercy promised to our fathers and to remember His holy covenant, the oath which He swore to our father Abraham; to grant us that we, being delivered from the hand of our enemies, might serve Him without fear, in holiness and righteousness before Him all the days of our life. And you, child, will be called the prophet of the Highest; for you will go before the face of the Lord to prepare His ways, to give knowledge of salvation to His people by the remission of their sins, through the tender mercy of our God, with which the Dayspring from on high has visited us; to give light to those who sit in darkness and the shadow of death, to guide our feet into the way of peace." ***So, the child grew and became strong in spirit, and was in the deserts till the day of his manifestation to Israel.*** *(Luke 1:57-80, NKJV)*

When it came time for his son to be circumcised, Zacharias experienced an anointing that came on him, and he began to prophesy.

His first prophecy was to the nation of Israel. It was a prophesy of remembrance. It was a prophesy referring to what Yahweh had already said about Israel. Yahweh would make a way of salvation for Israel from her enemies. As He had time and again in the past, Yahweh would provide salvation for the descendants of Abraham, Isaac, and Jacob.

Then Zacharias turned, and he prophesied directly to his son. Zacharias believed that this little baby could receive the prophetic word of Yahweh in his spirit. And John's spirit laid hold of that word. His mind did not understand a thing his father was saying the day of his circumcision, but his spirit received the prophetic word of his earthly father. From that day forth, John's life began to be shaped by that prophetic word.

There was a constraining force within John's spirit that held him back from some of the activities that a lot of other boys were involved in. In his spirit he knew he could not behave like his friends. Perhaps he wondered, *"Why am I not like other boys? Why don't I want to do the things they do? Why am I so unlike other people?"*

So, for many years John was constrained by the prophetic word of Yahweh that had been spoken by his father. John was constrained to remain in the desert while other boys were growing up, going off, and making their way in the world. While his contemporaries were trying to position themselves to make their mark in the world, John was in the desert.

John was never anxious out there because He came to understand that he was there by the constraining word of Yahweh, that he was there in Yahweh's time. He was there not until he reached a certain age; He was there until Yahweh said, "It is time to go."

The desert was John's preparation place for his purpose. It was in the desert that he was equipped. It was in the desert that he finetuned his communication with his Heavenly Father. It was in the desert that he learned to hear the Father's voice, and in that desert place, he learned to trust the voice he heard. In Luke 1:76-79, Zacharias prophesied about John bringing the good news of salvation to the people of Israel. John was to preach the remission of sins. Through his ministry, peace would be made available to all in Israel. In retrospect, the tasks with which John was charged do not seem radical, but in light of the times in which he lived, these messages would have been unique. Never had anyone dared to declare that sins could be forgiven in any other manner than by bringing acceptable sacrifices in an acceptable manner to the temple in Jerusalem. Never had anyone dared to declare that eternal salvation was available. Remember, the Jews were still under bondage to the law, and the system of the law precluded anyone from ever living a sin free life. A person had to continually receive remission of sins for transgressing the law. The concept of eternal salvation would have been completely foreign to the Jews in John's time. In fact, the concepts of remission of sins and eternal salvation were in direct contradiction to the law of the Jews. To preach something other than past revelation was to invite death. And nothing in John's background prepared him for the tasks with which he was charged. Remember, Zacharias was a priest, and he and his family would be well-acquainted with the law. Yet, John was charged to deliver these radical messages to Israel. He was charged to declare that Yahweh, the God of the patriarchal fathers, was declaring the old covenant void and was forming a new covenant with His people. To complicate matters, there was not a single person to whom John could turn to receive revelation on these topics. He could not sit at his earthly father's feet and learn of these matters from him. He could not go to the temple and learn from the high priest. He could not attend the next teaching convention held in Jerusalem's largest sports arena. There was only one place for John to be equipped to fulfill the purpose for which he was born – the desert. So, John went into the desert and received revelation that no one had ever heard before. While in the desert, he sat at the feet of his Heavenly Father and drew from His wisdom and knowledge. John was obedient to the constraining word of Yahweh to dwell in the desert. Now, John remained in the desert until the day of his manifestation to Israel, until the day he was revealed to Israel as the forerunner of the Messiah.

There then came a day when, like a meteor, he emerged flashing full of Yahweh's glory, full of His anointing. He did not start out and make the circuit in the little churches. He was not in anybody's church training school to be a prophet. He did not attend prophetic seminars to hone his anointing. His congregation and companions probably consisted of a few rabbits, gophers, and snakes; but he was faithful. He was not disillusioned. He knew he was in the right place. He knew he was on time because the living word of Yahweh was in his heart. John was content being a desert dweller, and he learned all he needed to know in order to fulfill his purpose in the desert. It was a safe place for him to grow, mature, and develop.

Now, look at another new testament believer. In Galatians, Apostle Paul tells the story how he became a desert dweller.

But I make known to you, brethren, that the gospel which was preached by me is not according to man. For I neither received it from man, nor was I taught it, but it came through the revelation of Jesus Christ. For you have heard of my former conduct in Judaism, how I persecuted the church of God beyond measure and tried to destroy it. And I advanced in Judaism beyond many of my contemporaries in my own nation, being more exceedingly zealous for the traditions of my fathers. But when it pleased God, who separated me from my mother's womb and called me through His grace, to reveal His son in me that I might preach Him among the Gentiles, I did not immediately confer with flesh and blood, ***not did I go up to Jerusalem to those who were apostles before me; but I went to Arabia......*** *(Galatians 1:11-17, NKJV)*

Remember what happened when Saul met Yahshua on the road to Damascus? He had that wonderful conversion experience and Yahweh began to speak to him about the tremendous ministry he was going to have. But for years, he did nothing. For fourteen years, believers heard that the one who had formerly persecuted them had joined them in their faith, but they had to receive this information by faith because Paul was not on the ministry circuit. He was not making appearances at the conventions and revival meetings. Paul, the mighty man of Yahweh, was in the desert for years and years and years and years of preparation for his purpose. There in the desert, Yahweh spoke to him. And everything Yahshua had spoken to Saul of Tarsus became a reality. Finally, one day, the church was in trouble, and Barnabas said, "I think I know a man that can help us." And he went and found Paul and brought him and introduced him into the ministry. And the rest is history.

Notice in the passage from Galatians that Paul, like John, received the message of the gospel, the message of the good news, by revelation. He did not hear it in school. He did not get it by conferring with someone else. The kingdom of Yahshua was revealed to him by revelation; and, Paul's response was to go to Arabia, the desert. Why? Why did Yahweh design a trip into Arabia, into the desert, for Paul? Because He was preparing Paul for a tremendous ministry. He did not send him down to some school of suffering. He did not send him to a seminary. He sent him into a desert place because there in the desert, Yahweh could reveal Himself. Yahweh could reveal His grace. Yahweh could reveal the gospel of Yahshua the Messiah to Saul of Tarsus, Saul a Pharisee – the one held in bondage by head knowledge of the Scriptures, the man who knew nothing about relationship with the Father. There in the Arabian desert, Yahweh, the God of Abraham, Isaac, and Jacob revealed Himself and His eternal plan to this Jewish man of learning. Yahweh took him away from all that he had ever known. He took him away from the scholars who knew the Scriptures but not the eternal God. He took him away from the Followers of the Way. He took him away from the apostles who had known Yahshua in the flesh. He took him away from everything in order to teach him all things.

Now, all desert dwellers did not live in Biblical times. Many who we will never know have lived in the centuries since the Scriptures were recorded. Some, of course, are alive today. Recently, I was reading a little biography of Paul Cain. Paul Cain is not a household name to most of us, but he has come to be recognized as a prophet of Yahweh to the body of Yahshua. I do not recall ever having heard of him, but as I read the little biographical sketch, I learned that he is a man about my age. His mother received a tremendous miracle of healing in order to give birth to him, and he was a supernatural child from the very beginning. He began a valid, legitimate ministry – preaching, holding evangelistic meetings, when he was nine years old. He had one of the biggest traveling tent ministries back in the 1950s.

And then Yahweh told him to leave the ministry and told him to remain celibate and take care of his mother. For years he shut himself away and did no ministry – supernatural birth, supernatural anointing but for years there was dead silence. Dead silence until years ago when Yahweh began to bring him out of the desert and began to send him supernaturally to world leaders. The word of Yahweh is sure, but it seldom is on the timetable that we envision in the beginning.

Many of my spiritual sons are present-day desert dwellers. When they leave their churches, their congregations, their ministries to come and sit in the congregation of the Rock of Panama City, they are usually entering the desert. They have heard the Father's voice to come here, and they are here out of obedience, but little will be heard from them for years. Many of their contemporaries will ask, "Whatever became of so-and-so? I do not hear anything about him anymore. Does anybody know what happened to him?"

This is a safe place, a place hidden away from much of the rest of the world. It is a place they can come to learn and be matured. The reason most of them come is because, after they have been in the ministry for a short period of time, they learn that they are not equipped. They have not been prepared to handle the day-to-day realities of functioning in the ministry.

I remember when Aaron Smith originally came to submit himself to me and this ministry. He thought he would be here about two years and then go to Pensacola and establish a work. Then one day he came to me and told me Yahweh had told him to lay that dream down and to make a commitment to remain here in Panama City, Florida. That prophetic word of Yahweh took all the striving out of him. It brought a rest to him, a confidence to him. Some people said, "Aaron went down to Panama City and could not get out of there. I heard about those big plans he had, how he was going to do great things over in Pensacola. I wonder what happened to him?" He went into the desert. One day, he heard the Father's voice say to him, "Go to Mobile. I have a place for you there. It is to that city that I have called you." And Aaron and Robbie and their children went to Mobile on a word from Yahweh and established The Rock of Mobile. So, Panama City was Aaron's desert place. It was here that he learned to rest. It was here that he learned to hear the Father's voice more clearly. It was here that he learned the importance of a relationship with the living, speaking God. It was here he learned how to receive revelation directly from the Father. It was here that he was prepared to possess his purpose.

I have had many desert experiences myself. I tell you I was as ignorant as a person could be when I received salvation. I already knew I was called into the ministry but getting saved did not enlighten me on how to get into the ministry. It just confirmed the call. But, in my ignorance, I began confessing that I was called into the ministry, and do you know what happened? I got fired. Within six weeks after we got saved, both my wife and I lost our jobs. We were a thousand miles from anybody who knew us. There was no one to help us. We had the usual debts incurred by a young couple and my wife was expecting our first child soon. If I had been going on appearances, I would have said I was backing up fast, that somehow this kingdom living was not what I had been told it was going to be.

Now I could have avoided all of the turmoil if I had not said anything about the dream in my heart. But, like Joseph, I did not have any better sense than to declare what was in my heart. What was in my heart came out of my mouth and got me into trouble because my bosses wanted men who were company men. They wanted men who would dedicate their lives to the company and I had other plans. But getting fired is what Yahweh used to separate me from the company and unto Him. We had Yahweh, and He turned what appeared to be a loss – around. He used it as an open door. He used it to help me make up my mind about some things.

One time I heard a pastor (who was in a religious system where they vote on pastors) say, "Getting voted out will help you make up your mind." Sometimes pastors debate with themselves or their families, "Should I stay, or should I go?" Sometimes the congregation will help you make up your mind in a situation like that; but do not fear if someone helps you make up your mind in a similar fashion. Our Heavenly Father has a way of opening the doors He wants opened in our lives. He has a way of allowing us to run into His desert to be prepared for what he wants us to do next.

I remember one particularly low point where Shirley, the children, and I had nowhere to go, and nobody was beating down the door to get to us. We had no name or reputation. With a sound of near hopelessness, Shirley asked, "What are we going to do?" My response was,

I do not know. The only thing I know for sure is Yahweh called me to preach. That is the only thing I know for sure. I do know that, and I am not backing up on that. I am holding onto that word.

Yahweh used that opportunity to lead me out of my present wilderness into His desert place.

Some years ago, I was an officer in a large denomination where I was respected by the people. I would frequently drive away from meetings where there had been hundreds of pastors with tears running down my face asking, "Yahweh, why do I feel so lonely? Why do I feel so left out?" Then I remember saying, "Yahweh, if being separated from these men, not being a part of what they are doing, means being joined to you, then so be it." During that time, I experienced a loneliness of people but such a blessed presence of Yahweh, and I began to understand some things about Yahweh's desert places, His preparations. Quite simply, it does not matter what people think. It does not matter whether they think you are on schedule or not. When you are in the desert, you have the confidence that you are walking out the will of Yahweh, and Yahweh has everything under control, and He is going to bring it to pass. He is going to bring it to pass. Yahweh is going to bring it to pass in your life. Hallelu-Yah!

Over the years, Holy Spirit has given me understanding of what is happening in the Church today, and how things fit together. He has also given me some understanding of things to come. But you will not read about it in Charisma magazine, and you will not hear about it on anybody's tape because these are things that I have never heard anyone else say. I have said, "Why have you frustrated me?" Have you ever believed that Yahweh deliberately frustrates you? He gives you a desire and you cannot make it work. He gives you a dream and no matter what you do, it just will not happen, and you feel frustrated! Many times I have felt an inner frustration. "Yahweh, if you were going to show me these things, why did you not give me a platform? Why did you stick me down here in Panama City? You do not go through this city going anywhere. Panama City is on the way to nowhere. I have felt many times as if I am from nowhere. I love this city, but sometimes in the Spirit it is like nowhere. Problems and doctrines and teachings that cause trouble in other churches never cause trouble here. We are too isolated. The problems never even get here. Pastors all over the country are worried about this and worried about that. We are never worried about those things. Because we are so isolated, it never gets here!

One Saturday night after prayer, I was sharing with someone some of the frustration that I sometimes feel. "Why, Yahweh, have you put these things in my heart and given me no platform, given me no voice?" That person responded, "Pastor I know that your time is coming soon." And immediately the Holy Spirit spoke to me about the prophetic word of Zacharias over John. Zacharias turned to that newborn baby and began to prophesy to him (Luke 1:76, KJV), *"And thou, child...."*

By the prophetic word he spoke over his son, Zacharias set the course and direction for John's life and ministry. Then *"the child grew, and waxed strong in spirit, and was in the deserts till the day of his showing unto Israel"* (Luke 1:80, KJV). There came a day. There came a time when Yahweh said, "John because you have been faithful to remain in the desert to preach to the few now, because you have been faithful, I will enable you to declare to multitudes the things that I have shown to you in the secret place.

That evening became a marked night for me because that was the time, I understood that Yahweh had placed me in Panama City precisely because it was isolated, expressly because it was a separate place designed and ordered so that I would not be drawn into or caught up with what other ministries were doing. Yahweh brought me to Panama City because it is my desert place. It has been the place He has matured me. It is the place where He has prepared for me to fulfill my call. But, like John, one day He will give me a platform from which I can speak all that He has spoken to me. When he does, I will be ready. I will be prepared.

I tell you that the word of Yahweh to you – the individual word, the individual dream that Yahweh has put into your heart is a living reality, if you will live like a desert person. Your day will come; your hour will come. Yahweh will vindicate you. Yahweh will establish you. He will put you over, if you keep your heart right and remain in the desert until He says, *"Go, now."* Until then, remain in the desert He has prepared for you.

CHAPTER SIX
WARNINGS ABOUT THE DESERT

You think the desert is without dangers, let me remind you that although it is a safe place, it is not some form of utopia. Remember, Satan is out to steal, kill, and destroy. He is roaming the earth seeking whom he may devour. The devourer is not banned from the desert. Just as there are natural dangers in a geological desert, there are spiritual dangers all desert dwellers need to take note of.

First of all, anybody who dwells in the desert needs the prophetic word of Yahweh for his life. Of course, the prophetic word does not always have to come from a prophet or prophetess. A prophetic word from Yahweh can come to you personally. Someone else does not have to get up and say, "I say unto thee…. Yea, thus saith Yahweh…" Now it is certainly acceptable if it comes that way, but the prophetic word of Yahweh is simply a definitive word from the Creator that communicates to you regarding His purpose and plan for you and it brings you rest.

Unequivocally, every person in every circumstance needs the prophetic word of Yahweh. Having a prophetic word of Yahweh removes all striving. You see, if you do not have a word from Yahweh, you are going to be striving. You are going to be striving to please people because you are believing that your promotion comes from people. You, therefore, must strive. You must do well. You must succeed. You must get ahead. When you are striving to do and to be, you are not living by the prophetic word of Yahweh. You are living by the word of people. You are believing that people's approval is what will elevate you. "Boy, I must please them. I must please my parents. I must please my teachers. I must please my employer." Now certainly, you ought to please them, but if you are striving to please them, you are going about it backwards. Instead of pursuing purpose, you are pursuing approval and recognition.

Whenever you receive a prophetic word of Yahweh, and you receive the partial fulfillment of that word, do not ever think that is all there is. Receive the partial fulfillment of the prophetic word as a token of the greater fulfillment. Some people are looking for a million dollars, and when they get a hundred thousand dollars, they quit looking. If Yahweh has placed in your heart a million dollars and you get a hundred thousand, do not receive that hundred thousand as though it were the million. Remember the promise, the fullness of the promise of Yahweh. Receive the hundred thousand as the assurance that the entire amount is coming to you. Do not quit believing. Do not get angry because you did not get the million. The one hundred thousand is a down payment on it. It is a partial fulfillment of the prophetic word of Yahweh. Hold onto that. Receive it, but receive it as the earnest of Yahweh, the assurance that the whole thing for which you believed Him is coming to pass.

Seldom, if ever, does a person receive the fullness of the inheritance of Yahweh in a single completion. There are steps in the prophetic word of Yahweh. Whenever the word of Yahweh comes to you, it will almost never be fulfilled in a single instance, a single day, a single moment. You need to remember that. Do not take a part of the fulfillment of Yahweh and then assume that is all there is. See what the greater prophetic word is because every obedience to the prophetic word of Yahweh releases Him to bring a part of that prophetic word to pass. When you receive part of that prophetic word, receive it as a confirmation of the validity of the word that you have already received and receive it as a promise of the greater fulfillment. When Yahweh says something to you, begin to watch for it. Be directed and guided by the prophetic word of Yahweh.

Go through the Scriptures. Not one person that I know ever received the fullness of the prophetic word of Yahweh in a moment. It came in degrees. It came as that person received part of it and then was faithful in continuing his walk with the Father. Follow Jacob. Follow Joseph. Follow Moses. Follow any of the Old Testament characters especially where we are given a sizeable biography, and you will find that the prophetic word of Yahweh never was fulfilled in a moment. When our Biblical counterparts set out to believe Yahweh for the whole, they received it in partial payments, but the partial payment was never viewed as being the fulfillment. They must have said, "Thank you, Yahweh, now where is the rest of it?" Look, that is not unthankfulness. That is faith. That is saying, "Father, I thank you for this loaf, but I believed you for the whole bakery. Now where is the bakery? I am not going to be satisfied with the loaf. You put into my heart the whole bakery. I appreciate the loaf, and I am going to eat it and enjoy it, but I am believing for the bakery itself."

Do not take partial payments as the fulfillment. Do not quit believing. Maintaining faith for the word of Yahweh to manifest in your life is not being unthankful.

If you promised your little boy a wagon, and in order to test him, you brought out a little red wagon that had no wheels on it, you would wonder about him if he said, "Thank you, Daddy, for the wagon!" and went running off to play with the wagon without wheels. No, he would say, Daddy, where are the wheels? Where is the rest of it? I believed for the *whole* wagon, and, Daddy, I want a *whole* wagon. I do not want just the wagon bed, I want the wheels, too." Yahweh wants you to believe him the same way. When He promises you something, He expects you to anticipate receiving exactly what He promised. He does not expect you to be content with less than what He promised prophetically.

If you get a letter or a phone call from someone you have reason to put trust in, and they say, "I have mailed you a package," guess what you are going to begin doing? You are going to begin paying attention to those you expect to deliver that package. You are going to set yourself in agreement with the word that has come to you and you begin to pay attention. You see, I do not go home every day and ask, "Did we get a package today? "Why? Because I am not expecting one. But if somebody called and said, "Today I mailed a package to you," when I went home the next day, I would ask Shirley, "Did we get that package?" If we did not get it, I would not say, "Liars! They promised me a package and it is not coming." No, I would say, "Well, it is coming Tuesday." When I came home Tuesday I would inquire, "Did we get the package?" Why? Because I am in agreement with the prophetic word. I have set myself in agreement.

You must pay attention when you receive a word from Yahweh and come into agreement with that word. Then when the partial fulfillment comes, do not just assume that is all there is. Start looking for more. Little children almost never believe that what you have given them is

Desert or Wilderness

the end of it. They ask expectantly, "What else do you have, Daddy?" Well, Yahweh says in some ways we are to be like children. Yet, some people have the craziest religious ideas about Yahweh. They are going around destitute, broken down. There is nothing going right for them, and they say, "Well, there are so many people so much worse off than I am, and I just would not want to ask Yahweh for anything." Honey, it will not bankrupt the Creator of the universe to provide for you! I am reminded of a story about two boys. One of them was wishing he had this, that, and the other. Standing by him, the other boy asked, "Man, if you had that, would you give me some of it?" And the first one answered, "No, you can wish, too!"

Now many of you may not believe that prophecy works, but I am telling you that all of you are prophets. You are today what you prophesied you were going to be yesterday. You are exactly where you prophesied you would be, so if you are in a bad place, just go back and look at what you prophesied. "Ah, nothing will ever work out for me. If I did not have bad luck, I would not have any luck at all. Everything is going backwards." Well, you can change that. You can come into agreement with the word of Yahweh. You can get a word from Him and come into agreement with that, and you will begin to prosper – if that is what you begin to prophesy. You see, Yahweh wants to get into agreement with you, but He is not going to get into agreement with you when you are prophesying gloom, doom, despair, heartache, and misery. He does not get into agreement with anybody who prophesies those things. But there is a spirit, there is one who will get into agreement with you. There is a deceiver. There is a destroyer. There is a devourer. There is a killer. There is a thief loose in the world, and he will come into agreement with you if that is what you want to prophesy.

One of the prophetic words you need to receive is knowledge of your purpose. You need to know what you were born to do. You need to know what Yahweh has called you to do and be. You need to move through life with a confidence, the confidence that is born out of knowing the will of Yahweh for you personally. You do not have to be trying to get ahead of people. That is not what a child of Yahweh does. He does not strive. He rests. He rests in Yahweh. You see, when Yahweh gives you His word, He then becomes responsible to fulfill His word. His responsibility is to make His word come true. Your responsibility is believing and resting. Believers do not have to struggle to make the word of Yahweh come true. He makes His word come true. Believers can rest in the desert because the Heavenly Father has brought them to this place for a purpose.

However, when you begin to talk about your dreams and the anointing becomes evident on you, you will become a threat to those who have the position to which you are called. When you begin to walk in the visions of Yahweh, when you begin to walk in the preparations of Yahweh, those who are in the positions of authority for which Yahweh has birthed you and anointed you are going to recognize that anointing. They are going to know that they do not rightfully belong. They are going to rise up and do their best to come against you and destroy you one way or another. When they cannot cajole you, when they cannot persuade you, they will rise up and try to destroy you. Remember what frightened Herod? There was a child born for the position that he held. Even though the Messiah was just a baby, Herod was afraid, and he tried to kill him. A similar situation happened with King Saul and Jesse's young son, David. David has this ability to play and drive the tormenting devils away from Saul, and Saul recognized that, but he also recognized something else. He recognized that this boy was anointed to be king and Saul was king, although Yahweh had taken His anointing off of Saul, and placed it on David. Every time David came into Saul's presence, the king was throwing a javelin trying to nail him to a wall. Why? Because Saul recognized the anointing, and he wanted to kill the one who had been anointed to take his place. I want to tell you that those who have bought, stole, or illegally gotten the position to which you are called will be threatened by your presence, and they are not going to bless you. They will recognize that Yahweh has anointed you for their job, that you were birthed for their position. Now, they may not know what to call the anointing they see on you, but they will identify you as a threat. They will not be glad to see you. They will reject you. They will do their utmost to kill you as we must be aware that the thief comes only to steal and kill and destroy.

So you must be aware of the messengers of death who have been sent to kill the word you have received, the word you are speaking. Do not respond to their threats. Do not react to their taunts. Just believe Yahweh. You may have to run as David did into the desert, but do not fight. Let Yahweh take care of it. Let Yahweh take care of your enemies. Yahweh knows how to put you where you are supposed to be at the right time. Just stay in the desert with Him. David spent some time down in what was described as wilderness country, but it was a desert place with David because it was Yahweh's preparation place for him, and he refused to take matters into his own hands because he trusted Yahweh. The day came when Saul was no longer standing in David's way. He died at his own hands, and Yahweh opened the door for David to become that for which he had been anointed many years before to do.

Also, beware that when you begin to speak the prophetic word of Yahweh to you that false accusations will be levied at you. And not all of these accusations will come from unbelievers. When you are going through trouble because of obedience, guess what the carnal believer is going to say? Guess what the unbeliever is going to say? Guess what your enemies are going to say? "Ah, ha! He is in trouble because of his disobedience." That is exactly what Job's friends did. Why did they make that kind of judgment? Because they were basing their judgment of Job on what they thought they knew.

One of the most difficult things that some people have to bear is the fact that they take seriously what other people say about them. I suppose we need to care what other people think about us – to a point, but do not stretch that point. Trust that there is no arrogance in my own heart when I tell you that it really does not matter very much to me what you think about me. I simply want to be able to look into the face of Yahweh and know I have been obedient to Him. I want to be able to look into the secret places of my own heart and know that with the help of Yahweh, I have been as right as I know how to be, that I have done the best that I know how. Now, if you do not come to the decision I came to about caring what others think or say, you are going to live in some hard places in life because your enemies and carnal believers are never going to be able to make spiritual discernment about what you are going through.

If you want to be reminded what it is like when you are in trouble because of obedience, to have your friends misunderstand you, read again the book of Job. Everybody had an opinion about why Job was going through difficulty, but the truth is no one had spiritual discernment. Even Job himself did not fully discern or fully understand, but you and I are living in a better time than Job. So, as far as we know, Job is the oldest book in the Bible and Job certainly did not have the opportunity of the light, the understanding, the relationship, the ministry of Holy Spirit, or the written word of Yahweh that you and I have today. So,

Job can be excused if he did not understand, but there is no excuse for you and me.

Above all else, the desert experience is characterized by knowing the will of the Father, knowing that you are in the desert because you have been obedient to His word – not man's expectations of you, and resting in the word of the Creator's awesome power. While in the desert, do not allow anyone or anything to draw you away from Yahweh's rest.

CHAPTER SEVEN
HOW TO RESPOND IN THE DESERT

Here are some simple helps for desert people. As I have said before, the desert is Yahweh's place of preparation. It is where Yahweh is preparing you for what He is calling you to do. While a believer does not spend all of his life in the desert, there are desert periods in every believer's life. Certainly, these periods of preparation are necessary and desirable, and demonstrating a proper response to being in the desert is vital to every believer who wants to possess his promised land – his purpose.

So, what should be the response for the person who finds himself in a desert place because of obedience? The immediate response should be to rejoice. One simple word sums it all up. When you find that you are in the desert, when you find that you are in trouble because of your obedience to Yahweh, your response should be to rejoice.

First of all, you know that you are there because of obedience. Therefore, your Heavenly Father has obligated Himself to care for you in that circumstance. Consequently, His word that no waters shall drown you and no fire shall leave its mark on you is activated because of your obedience to Him (Isaiah 43:2, NKJV). Now, it may look to other people as though you are in a wilderness situation, that you are in a terrible conflict. And you are in a conflict. But you are rejoicing, because what appears to some people to be a terrible, destructive thing in your life, is the will and the purpose of Yahweh, and you recognize that you are in His desert place.

You see, you cannot always control the events in your life. What you can control is your response to those events. Some people get thrown into prison, and every day is a nightmare. Every day is a horrible experience. Other men have been thrown into prison, and every day is an opportunity of ministry. They just simply realize the Yahweh has changed their place of ministry. He has changed the opportunity, but they see their slavery as an opportunity to serve Yahweh.

James issued an admonition to the early church to behave in a similar fashion:

James, a servant of God and of the Lord Jesus Christ, to the twelve tribes which are scattered abroad: Greetings. My brethren, count it all joy when you fall into various trails, knowing that the testing of your faith produces patience. But let patience have its perfect work, that you may be perfect and complete, lacking nothing. If any of you lacks wisdom, let him ask of God, who gives to all liberally and without reproach, and it will be given to him. But let him ask in faith, with no doubting, for he who doubts is like a wave of the sea driven and tossed by the wind. For let not that man suppose that he will receive anything from the Lord; he is a double-minded man, unstable in all his ways. (James 1:1-8, NKJV).

Now James says when you are in trouble count it joy. Rejoice if you are in trouble because of obedience. If you look into your heart and say, "Yahweh, to the very best of my ability, to the very best of my understanding, I have wholly followed you." Then you can know that whatever difficulty you are facing has come because of your obedience. Why? Because you are there due to obedience. Therefore, you are Yahweh's responsibility, and He never fails. He never loses a case. So, count it all joy.

Apostle Paul had some experiences like that. There were times when he was in jail. There were times when Paul was in the depths of the sea. There were times when he was being stoned, but he said, "I count it all joy." Why? Because with unshakable conviction, he knew in the depths of his spirit that he was there because he had obeyed his Savior. He was not in those circumstances because of disobedience. He was not there because he wanted to run against the will of his maker. He was not there because he had gotten out of Yahweh's timing. He was walking in those experiences with total confidence and peace because he was there in obedience to the will of His loving Father.

Once you find yourself in Yahweh's desert, the next response you should make after rejoicing is to keep your heart with all diligence. Do not ever let bitterness, resentfulness, anger, or blame toward others (or secret blame toward Yahweh) get into your heart. It is so easy to say, "Well, Yahweh, you promised. You promised. I have declared this, and I have declared that, because that is what You said to me. And You have not done these things I have declared. Now I am embarrassed because these things have not come to pass, and I have all of these problems, and all of these enemies have risen up against me, and so forth."

If you are not careful, you will allow poison to get into your heart and absolutely destroy Yahweh's ability to do what He promised to do for you.

So, *keep your heart with all diligence, for out of it spring the issues of life* (Prov. 4:23, NKJV). I tell you there is nobody important enough for me to hate, because hating them would rob me of realizing of my dream. Nobody is important enough for me to spend my time defending myself against that person. I refuse to allow anyone to hurt me for any reason. You see, people cannot offend you unless you receive offense. People cannot hurt you unless you receive hurt. Just imagine that what has been done to you had been done to someone else. Would you be hurt about it? Would you be offended? Just imagine that what was being said had been said by someone other than the person who said it. Would you receive offense? I am certain some of you are rising up saying, "But, Pastor, you do not understand." Oh, I understand. I understand that you need to make a choice not to allow anyone to offend you. Do not allow anyone to reject you, in the sense that you are hurt by their rejection. You see, if I keep my heart right, nobody can keep me from receiving the blessing of Yahweh. All the powers of darkness and all of my enemies might stand and rise up and call me cursed and call me a fool, but they cannot keep me from receiving my inheritance if I keep my heart right. By the grace of Yahweh, as long as I am in the desert, I am going to keep my heart right.

In this matter, we should be like the Thessalonians Paul was commending in Thessalonians.

We are bound to thank God always for you, brethren, as it is fitting, because your faith grows exceedingly, and the love of every one of you all abounds toward each other, so *that **we ourselves boast of you among the churches of God for your patience and faith in all your persecutions and tribulations that you endure,** which is manifest evidence of the righteous judgment of God that you may be counted worthy of the kingdom of God, for which you also suffer; since it is a righteous thing with God to repay with tribulation those who trouble you, and to give you who are troubled rest with us when the Lord Jesus is revealed from heaven with His mighty angels, in flaming fire taking vengeance on those who do not know God and on those who do not obey the gospel of our Lord Jesus Christ. (2 Thess. 1:3-8, NKJV)*

You see, these people were doing what James wrote about and instructed us to do in James 1:1-8. What were they doing? They were exercising patience and faith. Where? In church on Sunday morning? No, in all their persecutions and tribulations. Why were they in persecutions? Why were they in tribulations? Because of obedience.

A few years ago, my wife and I were invited to meet with a group of pastors and their wives in another state. Most of these people had formerly been in membership in the same organization of which we had spent most of our ministry. When we left that meeting, I remarked to Shirley, "I really feel sorry for these men and their wives." Almost without exception, they were carrying hurt. They felt that they had been wronged by the denomination. They allowed other people to inflict hurt on them. There is always opportunity to receive hurt and to receive offense if you will receive it; but I want to encourage you today to make the decision not to receive offense from anyone. Do not receive hurt from anyone. Instead, understand that because you have followed Yahshua the Messiah, some people will be unhappy with you. But even when they rise up against you, and you find yourself caught between two opposing forces – the pull of the kingdom on the one hand, and the pull of friends and the pull of family on the other – make the determination that you will rejoice.

Your dream, your vision, your call will turn what people call a wilderness into a preparation place if you keep your heart right, if you will use the opportunity to praise and worship the living, speaking God. Do not curse the work. Do not curse the things you have to do, because you can turn Yahweh's preparation place into a wilderness experience if you do not keep a right attitude. Do your best. Become one who praises and worships Yahweh wherever you are.

Rejoice and keep your heart right, as young David did. David was a shepherd boy. I suppose he was the family's shepherd because, like Joseph, he was young in the family and the other boys were off doing important tasks. So, David was taking care of the dumb sheep. Notice again how important it is how you do what you do, how you receive what you receive. Most people view their job as a reflection of who they are and what they are. *Well, my bosses have me doing this job. They must not think very much of me. Anybody could do this job. It is a dirty job, a stinking job, a no good job. I am better than this. I am going to look for another job.*

The job needs to take on a different character. Whatever you are doing, you need to do it as though it were the most important thing being done. If you are cleaning toilets, the toilets you clean should be the cleanest ones in town. Do not allow the job you are doing to dictate how you feel about yourself. Why not turn the tables? Why not say, "I am important. Yahweh has called me. This is a preparation time in my life. I know I am not going to be doing this all of my life." Be faithful over little things. So many people are waiting for the big opportunity, and they never get the big opportunity because they are always looking for that, and they never apply themselves to what is at hand. Whatever you are doing, take the attitude: *It must be important; they have me doing it. They would not waste me. Surely, they recognize my talents, my ability. They have me doing very important work here, so I am going to do it like the important work it is.* And guess what? Your supervisor probably will begin to notice that you treat work like it is important, and like it is worth being done right, and he will begin to pay attention. And Yahweh will use that to elevate you, to promote you, like He elevated young David.

There came a time when the anointing of Yahweh came on David. Samuel came down to Jesse's house, and surely young David thought, "Boy, I must be important. I am big time now." David probably felt like his day had come, but it had not. Then when he was introduced to the king he probably thought, "My time is here. Things are rolling now." But the king recognized the anointing on him, and the king identified him as a threat. What did David do? Did he allow hatred and bitterness to rule his heart? No, he had compassion for Saul and refused to lift his hand against him. David kept his heart pure before his God.

Do not become bitter in the desert. Do not become cynical. Do not lose faith in people or yourself. Just say, "This is Yahweh's preparation. This is Yahweh's desert." Make the decision to remain faithful. Decide to do the best job anybody has ever done in your circumstance. Let the resolve of your heart be, *I do not care if I am assigned to pick up sticks, I am going to pick them up and pile them up neater than anybody ever did before. I am going to be faithful. I do not care what people say. They can criticize. They can reject. But I have heard the word of Yahweh. I am not in a wilderness because of disobedience. I am in a desert because I have heard Yahweh's word, and I am laying hold of it, and I am obeying.*

Yahweh's people are prepared in desert places. They get there when they hear the word of Yahweh, and they lay hold of the word of Yahweh. They are rejected by those who do not understand, but they are received by Yahweh. I doubt that David became weary of being in the desert once he understood he was there out of obedience, he was out there so he could be prepared to inherit his rightful position, and all the while he rejoiced and kept his heart right.

Then, the next thing you need to do when you find yourself in the desert is to keep on praying. What do you do out in the desert? You rejoice, first of all, then keep your heart right, and then pray and ask Yahweh for wisdom. When you are going through difficulty, that is the time to ask Yahweh for wisdom. What is wisdom? It is Yahweh's understanding, His knowing why and how and everything about the circumstance you are in.

You see, one of the first things I look for when I am in trouble is my own heart. Have I missed Yahweh's timing? Have I missed Yahweh's will somehow? I do not want to take for granted that everything I do is always in perfect agreement with Yahweh. I want it to be but I know that sometimes it is not. So, when I am in a difficult place I step back and say, "Holy Spirit, teach me, show me. Did I leave a door open? Did I make a wrong turn in the road? Did I get out of Yahweh's timing?

Let me share this little insight with you. Seldom has Yahweh ever given me what I needed when I asked for it. Even the solutions for problems about which I am praying have seldom come in a flash of lightning as I am praying. But I have found if I will lay them before the Heavenly Father and if I will continue to pray about them (but not pester Yahweh about them), He will answer me suddenly when I am not even thinking about the problems.

I got into an awful predicament a few years ago. I hired two people because I continually pestered Yahweh about whether or not to hire the men. Finally, He said, "Do whatever you want to." So, I put the men on staff but shortly thereafter, I began to suspect that I had made a mistake. And from that experience I learned not to nag my Heavenly Father! After I went to Him and asked where I had erred, He showed me that what I had done was no different than when a child comes to a parent and says, "Daddy, I want to do something." The father answers, "No, I do not think that is a good idea." Then the child begs, "Daddy, I want …… Daddy, I want….. Daddy, I want…. Daddy…." Finally, the father says, "Go do what you want to!" It is not the father's will nor is it best for the son. So, the father allows his son to go ahead and do whatever is in his young heart hoping that next time the child will learn to listen to him. In the same manner, sometimes our Heavenly Father gets frustrated when we continue to pester Him about something. Sometimes He says, "Yes," not because it is His perfect will but because He is trying to teach us to trust Him and His wisdom. I have learned if you pester or nag Yahweh, you are going to get into trouble. If you seek for a word, you are going to get a word, and it will probably not be the word of Yahweh. It will be a word that you conjure up out of your own spirit, out of your own desires. And it will get you in the wilderness. It will get you into trouble.

When you are in the desert, do not pester Yahweh for a word. Simply pray. Ask for wisdom. Job could have saved himself a lot of trouble and his friends could have saved themselves a lot of trouble if they had asked, "Yahweh, what is going on here?" However, it is so much easier to assume that we know what is going on. And if you are not careful, you will begin to have an opinion about why you are in trouble, and you will begin to try to figure it out.

It is not enough to know what Yahweh wants. You also need to know *when and where* and how and *with whom*. All of those questions are factors in the will and purpose of Yahweh in your life. So, when you are in difficulty, ask Yahweh for wisdom. Do not start making decisions. Do not start opinionating, and for goodness sakes, do not ask everybody else what you should do.

Let me say this to you. When you are going through trouble, first of all ask Yahweh for wisdom in your own heart, in your own spirit. Then, if you feel the need, go to those whom Yahweh has set over you in the ministry and share your situation and ask them by the Holy Spirit to give you counsel. But when you have received counsel, do not run to everybody else and talk to them about your problem. You are muddying the waterhole a little bit more. I know you want to talk. I know you are frustrated. I know you are angry. I know you are hurt but keep silent. Just shut up. Be quiet. Walk out obedience to the counsel you have received. Everybody has an opinion about your problem. Everybody has an opinion about what you should do. But nobody has to accept the consequence of what you do. See, it is easy for people to say, "Well, I will tell you right now what I would do…." Oh, yes, but they are not going home where you are going home. And they are not working where you work, and they are not in the circumstance you are in. It is easy to make decisions about somebody else's problem. It is easy to solve any problem if you are thinking only about the now. But what about the consequence of this decision?

When there is trouble, some people say, "I am going through such a hard time. I just do not feel like praying." Look, that is the time you grab yourself by the scruff of the neck and say, "Get out of that man!" That is when you need to talk mean to yourself.

"Get up and pray, Nolan!"

"But I don't want to."

"Get up."

"I'm tired."

"Get up."

"Don't you know I have problems?"

"Get up!"

"No, I do not want to."

"Get up and pray now!"

Everyone that prays has to make a decision to pray. Get into agreement with Yahweh. Receive the word of Yahweh. And pray until you breakthrough. Now, I will confess. Sometimes, when I get up in the morning, it takes all I can do to pray. And some days when I pray, my prayers sound as tired as my body. But I am not moved by how I sound. I am not moved by what I feel at the moment. I know if I am faithful to sow in prayer, the revelation of the Spirit of Yahweh is going to come. Seldom do the answers ever come while I am praying about the answers, but if I am faithful in prayer, Yahweh will always be faithful, perhaps not in my time, but in His time. And I have decided to make my time, His time, so do not hurry me. Do not rush me.

One thing I have learned about prayer is never to seek a word *for* someone. That is risky business. And I have a word of advice for you; do not seek a word *from* someone. I do not ever seek a word from Yahweh for myself anymore. I seek only Him and His wisdom. I try to keep an ear open to my Father's voice; I try to have my spirit set to hear the Master's voice. Then whenever Yahweh wants to talk to me, my lines of communication are open. I have learned when you begin seeking Yahweh for a particular thing, there are going to be many voices crying out for your attention. There are going to be many, many voices coming to you with many suggestions. And there are going to be voices of temptation "Go this way. Do this. Do this now." So, keep praying for Yahweh's wisdom. Once you have received His wisdom about a situation, you will know the *who, what, where, when, and how* of His plan.

Do not judge by man's timetable. Do not go by man's watch; go by the Eternal Timekeeper's clock. Go by Yahweh's timetable. He will put His word in your heart. Pray. Seek Yahweh. Do not worry about His will. Do not worry about *the how, the when, the why, the where, the who.* Just continue to seek Yahweh. He will put it together.

When you find yourself in the desert, continue to rejoice; keep your heart pure; continue praying, asking for wisdom. And do not change direction. Whatever you do, do not change direction. A double minded man says, "I will. I will not. I can. I cannot. I know. I am not sure. Yes. No." A double minded person is unstable in all of his ways, and he will end up in the wilderness.

Wilderness people go around in circles. If you do not believe that, get your Bible and look at the map in the back. Follow the wilderness wanderings of Israel. Around and around and around and around and around they went. And where they were, nobody knew. But people with a mission, people who are in the desert, do not wander aimlessly. They continually walk toward their purpose. It may not appear as if they are making much progress, but they tuck their chin into their chest, set their eyes on the finish line, and they walk toward their purpose until they reach it. John the Baptist was not constantly changing his address. For thirty years, he lived in the desert. He did not move into the city, then out into the country. He did not move out of the country, then into the city. No one asked, "Where's John?" They knew he was in the desert. Why? Because he was in the desert in the will of Yahweh. He was there in Yahweh's timing. He was there by the constraint of the Holy Spirit. He was not double minded. *I will. I will not. I believe Yahweh called me. I do not know. I think I am supposed to stay here. Maybe I am supposed to go.* Who would want to follow somebody like that?

You may not want to follow me, but at least you will know where I am going. "Where is Nolan Ball?" "He went that way." You will not be saying, "I do not know where he is. The last time I saw him he was going around and around and around and around." This ministry is not changing direction. I freely confess that The Rock of Panama City is not the church for all people. But I will tell you this, you will know whether or not it is the church for you. Why? Because by the anointing of the Spirit of Yahweh we have raised a standard. We know what we are called to do. We know what we are called to say. We know what we are called to be. We are not raising one standard and then another one.

When the tribes of Israel were assembled, they looked like several million unorganized people, but do you know how they achieved organization? They raised a standard. Somebody in Judah raised a standard for Judah and everybody who was from the tribe of Judah ran to that banner. Then Benjamin raised a standard, and all those from the tribe of Benjamin gathered together beneath Benjamin's standard. Each tribe raised a standard, and everybody ran to his own standard. That is what we have done here at The Rock of Panama City.

I have seen pastors who cannot make up their minds what they believe, who cannot make up their minds where they want to go, and they wonder why no one follows them. I know some churches that cannot decide if they are traditional or charismatic, whether they are Pentecostal, progressive, or conservative. They have one service at 8:00 for one group of people and another service at 10:00 for another crowd. That is trying to be all things to all people, and it is a bunch of nonsense. Then they wonder why nobody can decide who to follow. Because nobody has decided to lead. The size of the congregation at The Rock of Panama City will be determined by the number of people out there who decide they want to follow the standard that we have raised. But there will never be any ambiguity about that standard. It will not be flying for one crowd on the east and another crowd on the west. It will look the same no matter from which direction it is viewed. The standard will not be one thing this week and another thing next week. It will not be one thing at 8:00 and something else at 11:00. We know the direction in which we are going, and we will not change that direction.

You will remember that there is a story in the gospel about a time when Yahshua instructed his apostles to get into a boat and go to the other side of the lake of Galilee. Very quickly after they embarked on the journey, they encountered a fierce storm. In the natural realm, that is what you would expect, because in the spiritual realm, that is what always happens. When you set out to follow Yahweh, there will be a storm. Make no mistake about it. Just look for it. Go ahead. Batten down the hatches. Secure everything, because you will encounter a storm. Now the easy thing would have been to turn the boat around and let the wind drive it back into the port from which they had just departed. But the disciples did not take the easy way out. All night they toiled, but they never changed direction.

"Fellows, why not change direction?"

"Because Yahshua said, 'Go to the other side.'"

Desert or Wilderness

"Fellows, it would be a lot easier to go back into port."

"But Yahshua said, 'Go to the other side.'"

"Fellows, you are not making any progress!"

"But Yahshua said, 'Go to the other side.'"

Then the next morning when Yahshua finally came to them, where were they? They were not far into their journey as far as distance is concerned, but the boat was still headed toward the other shore! They were looking toward the other shore. And when Yahshua came, they were *immediately* transported to the other shore.

So, whatever you do when you set out to follow Yahweh and the storm comes, do not change direction. Do not get your boat crosswise with the current. Do not try to turn around in the storm. You will get swamped. You will get drowned. You will walk out of the desert into the wilderness if you change direction.

Learn to wait on Yahweh and do not quit. Do not give up in the desert. Although the desert is a good place, you can die in the desert. Learn to wait on Yahweh, His word to you, and His timing. Get this in your heart today – Yahweh's preparation places are not wilderness experiences. Yahweh's preparation places are deserts, and if you understand that, you can learn how to relax in the desert. You can learn how to abide, how to wait on Him and His word to you, and you will never give up on His purpose for your life.

I remember my uncle (who was a preacher) encouraged me to go to Bible school. I wonder what would have happened to me if I had immediately followed that uncle's suggestion. Most likely, I would have been caught up in some religious system. I would have been trained and nurtured along the way, and it would have seemed to be the right thing because it was right that I preach. But I would have been out of my Heavenly Father's time. Now I cannot explain to you why Yahweh waits. I cannot explain to you why He does not let us get on with the task to which we are called. But I believe there is a sovereignty of the Father's will. I believe there are divine appointments in life. And I believe that if somehow, we can be kept from rushing ahead of Him, Yahweh will order all aspects of our lives.

Let me share with you another personal example of how I waited on Yahweh about a particular situation. Over the years I have gone to a lot of seminars and most of them have had little good in them. But most of them can be described in this manner: you pay your registration, you buy your ticket, you travel to the meeting, and the advertised expert is delivered to the back door in a limousine with dark glasses. He comes through the back door onto the platform. He is called to stage with great introduction and proceeds to tell me about how great he is and what great things he has done. And if I will do like he has done, I, too, can have great success. Then, he never touches anybody. He never sits down with anybody. Instead, he goes out the same back door into the same limousine and he is treated like a Hollywood movie star.

I became weary of such meetings some years ago, so I began to say that I was tired of going to seminars. One day I told my wife, "If you ever hear me talking about going to another seminar, get a Louisville slugger and scramble my brains!" But often in talking to other people and sharing with them my dissatisfaction I would say, "I would fly across the country just to sit down with somebody under an oak tree and talk." I wanted to share what I was hearing and receiving by the Spirit and I wanted to draw from others what the Spirit was saying to them. So, over the years, I have meditated upon doing something like that and different people have encouraged me to schedule some meetings, to put something together, to get started on this project, but I never had a release from Holy Spirit to go forward with specific plans.

Then, a few years ago, I was doing some work out in my garage and had not thought about wanting to sit under an oak tree and talk to someone for quite a while. I was not praying about it, but Holy Spirit suddenly spoke into my spirit and said, "That is in the Bible." I sort of shook my head in confusion and asked, "What is in the Bible?" He said, "Sit under an oak tree; that is in the Bible and that is the theme for your dialogue; now is the time to begin it." So, I went to my concordance and was directed to two passages that refer to an angel sitting under an oak tree conversing with a man.

And there came an angel of the Lord, and sat under an oak which was in Ophrah, that pertained unto Joash the Abiezrite: and his son Gideon threshed wheat by the winepress, to hide it form the Midianites. (Judges 6:11, KJV)

And Gideon went in, and made ready a kid, and unleavened cakes of an ephah of flour: the flesh he put in a basket, **and he put the broth in a pot, and brought it out unto him under the oak, and presented it."** *(Judges 6:19, KJV)*

Here you have a picture of Gideon and the angel of Yahweh sitting under an oak tree talking about the will of Yahweh, about what Yahweh wanted to do. In places where there are deserts, or the land is barren, trees are very important. In many African villages, the largest tree in the village is an important place. It will almost become a sacred place, because it is where the village elders meet to confer together. Anything of any importance in an African village is going to take place under the tree. That was the kind of situation the Scriptures mention here in

Judges. The angel came and sat and talked to Gideon. Most likely, the angel did not have a chair, so he probably sat down on his haunches. That is humorous to me. Now that may not mean anything to you, but it is a wonderful confirmation to me that if you will wait on Yahweh in your desert place, He will bring to pass what you desire in your heart.

Out of a good desire Holy Spirit had planted in my heart, I could have gone ahead and started these dialogues many years ago, and the actions would have been right, but the timing would have been wrong. Furthermore, I would never have accomplished what Yahweh put into my heart to accomplish. However, once I had received Yahweh's word of direction, I began to organize some meetings like I had imagined in my spirit.

These dialogues are called *Under the Oak*. The idea is to come sit, and to talk together. Nobody knows it all. There is a five-fold ministry that needs to function together and there are many apostolic anointings in the earth that need to share with one another. We are not going to hear the word of Yahweh by some committee meeting in some headquarters of some denomination and come up with a program for the next five or ten years. Instead, we are going to discern the mind of Yahweh if we will sit down as elders one with another and invite the presence of the Eternal God to come and sit down under that tree with us and communicate to us what His Spirit is saying.

So, learn to wait on Yahweh in your desert places. If you are in trouble and you do not know that you are where you are because of obedience, you will become unraveled. In the Scriptures, the idea of waiting on Yahweh is likened to making a rope – taking many individual strands of a materials (hemp, cotton, nylon, etc.) and beginning to weave them together. When you have finished, you have a very strong rope. Waiting on Yahweh means that instead of going to pieces in times of stress or crisis, instead of becoming emotional and reacting to the circumstance, you are going to wait on His word, and He will show you how to weave the strands of your life together so that you become a strong, useful tool in His kingdom. Hold steadfast in the desert and do not be moved. Do not get on somebody's else's time schedule. Wait on Yahweh and do not quit.

Hebrews was written to a people who had started the Christian walk (really an Ironman Triathlon!) and then began to debate about whether they should continue. Now, the key to their continuing was hearing. They were never challenged to continue their journey based on what they had heard. They were encouraged to continue their journey based on what they were hearing each day – today, today, today. Today, *if you will His voice...* (Heb. 3:7, NKJV)

Let me say this to you, as the prophet of old learned, the voice of the living, speaking God may not come in the whirlwind; it may not come in the fire; it may, but it may not. It may come in the earthquake, but it may not. It may come by a still, small voice, but the reassuring voice of Yahweh will always come to those who find themselves in the desert and in the stormy place because of obedience to His word. So, set yourself to hear His voice today, today, today. We are not asked to live our Christian lives based on what Yahweh *said*. We are called to the challenge of living by what Yahweh keeps on *saying*. I thank Yahweh that He spoke decades ago. I thank Yahweh that He spoke years ago. But I want to tell you that the God who spoke then is still communicating to my heart today, still directing and leading. So, wait on Yahweh, just wait on Him.

If you do not quit, if you do not give up, if you do not change directions, one way or another, the voice of Yahweh will come through. And when you hear that voice, it will always be a voice of encouragement. Listen to these words out of *Hebrews 10:26-39.*

For if we sin willfully after we have received the knowledge of the truth, there no longer remains a sacrifice for sins, but a certain fearful expectation of judgment, and fiery indignation which will devour the adversaries. Anyone who has rejected Moses' law dies without mercy on the testimony of two or three witnesses. Of how much worse punishment, do you suppose, will he be thought worthy who has trampled the Son of God underfoot, counted the blood of the covenant by which he was sanctified a common thing, and insulted the Spirit of grace? For we know Him who said, "Vengeance is mine, I will repay," says the Lord. And again, "The Lord will judge His people." It is a fearful thing to fall into the hands of the living God. But recall the former days in which, after you were illuminated, you endured a great struggle with sufferings: partly while you were made a spectacle both by reproaches and tribulations, and partly while you became companions of those who were so treated; for you had compassion on me in my chains, and joyfully accepted the plundering of your goods knowing that you have a better and an enduring possession for yourselves in heaven. **Therefore, do not cast away your confidence, which has great reward. For you have need of endurance, so that after you have done the will of God, you may receive the promise:**

For yet a little while, and He who is coming will come and will not tarry. **Now the just shall live by faith; But if anyone draws back, My soul has no pleasure in him."** But we are not of those who draw back to perdition, but of those who believe to the saving of the soul.

You see, the only proper response to revelation is obedience. Sin is not limited to sins of the flesh. It may be sins of disobedience. What happens to the person to whom the Holy Spirit reveals the next step of Yahweh's plan in his life? Then, that person looks around them and says, "Oh, but, Yahweh, if I do this, my family will not understand. If I do this, my church will not understand. If I do this, my denomination will not understand." Can I tell you that it is just as sinful and just as disobedient for a person to refuse to walk in the light of the revelation truth of Yahweh as it is for a man to go out and commit adultery. Sin of any kind will lead you away from Yahweh. When you do not obey Yahweh, you are insulting His Holy Spirit. You are insulting Him. The Spirit of Revelation, Holy Spirit, comes with a message from Yahweh. He comes with a word to you, and you have the temerity to say, "No, no, no!"

So do not quit. Do not allow yourself to grow weary. Do not give up on the word of Yahweh. Do not quit. Yahweh's word is true. If you will be true, His word will come to pass in your life. Do not get impatient. The prophetic word of Yahweh will come to pass. It took about thirty years for John the Baptist to see Yahweh's word manifest. It took at least thirty years for Joseph. It took many years for David. It took at least fourteen years for Saul of Tarsus. But the prophetic word of Yahweh kept them steady and faithful during what we describe as their desert experience.

Learn to lay the matter before Yahweh. Rejoice in Him. You do not have to make His word to you come to pass. You do not have to create it. All you need to do is discern by the Spirit what He wants to do, and you believe, and begin to declare it. Sometimes in our ignorance we declare the word of the Lord, but we are declaring it out of a genuine, sincere desire – like when I would talk about sitting down under an oak tree. It was a desire in my spirit, a desire to talk with other people. I had something to say; they had something to say. I wanted to have an exchange with other ministers of the Word, and I have seen that word come to pass because I waited to hear *what, how, whom, when,* and *where*.

So, keep on saying. Keep on declaring. Do not let your testimony waiver. Keep on declaring. Mark 11 talks about verbally prophesying Yahweh's will to a circumstance, a mountain. The idea is that if you will keep on saying, if you will keep on releasing Yahweh's word in the earth, the circumstance will change, the mountain will come down. And once you have made your position clear, once you have heard the voice of the Spirit of Yahweh, once you have ascertained the direction Yahweh wants you to go, declare it with your mouth, and no matter what storms may roar, no matter what the critics may say, no matter what conventional wisdom may dictate, you are still declaring. You are still declaring. And guess what? Yahweh is pulling you onward with His prophetic word.

Revelation 12:11 speaks of a group of people who overcame the powers of the enemy by the blood of the Lamb and by the word of their testimony. James says a double-minded man, one who says one thing one day and something else the next, unstable in all of his ways, and that man shall not receive anything from Yahweh *(James 1:6-8)*. Now, a lot of people started out to receive a good inheritance from their Heavenly Father, but they became double minded. Their "Yes" was not always "Yes" and their "No" was not always "No". They vacillated. They changed directions and they got swamped by the storm. But those of us who keep on hearing and keep on declaring are going to receive everything Yahweh has ever spoke to us, even if we have to live as long as Methuselah. One of the reasons the first generations lived so long is that it took them that long to receive the promise of Yahweh. If I have to outlive Methuselah, I am going to see everything Yahweh has promised me because I am not quitting. I am not giving up. I will continue to prophesy the word Yahweh has placed in my heart. I have not backed up today. I am not changing one bit because of time. I am not moved by what I see or what I do not see. I am moved only by the word of Yahweh.

You, too, must declare the prophetic word Yahweh has given you. You must be a little bit like Joseph. Now, you and I can argue about whether or not it was wisdom for Joseph to share his dream with his brothers, but let me say this, no dream will ever become a reality until you are willing to put it on the line. Until you are willing to declare out of your own mouth what you intend to do and be, you will never move toward the fulfillment of it.

Now if you are thinking, "Well, I do not want any trouble, and I do not want anybody misunderstanding me, so I am just going to dream my dreams in my heart. Yahweh and I will work it out." No, you see, He responds to words, spoken words, words that come out of human mouths; and, when you dare to put the dream in your spirit into words that can be heard and interpreted (or misinterpreted) by other people, then He will begin the formation and the realization of your dream. But until you declare it, it will not manifest in your life. I would not be in the ministry today if I had not stood and declared. You know, in my ignorance, I thought somebody would be happy. I thought somebody would rejoice with me. I am telling you nobody was happy when I told them I was called to preach. My wife was very cooperative. She said, "Well, whatever." My pastor just looked at me with a blank stare. Nobody got excited about it. I do not think anybody believed it but me and Yahweh.

I might have been like the man who was working back during WWII when the government had people frozen on their jobs. If a job was considered to be essential to defense purposes, you could not leave your job. Well, this man got the idea that he was called to preach, so he went to his foreman and said, "Sir, this is a wartime effort. You cannot get out of this job. You must stay here. Why do you want to leave, anyway?" His employee answered, "I have been called to preach." And the foreman responded, "I am sorry about that, but as long as the war is going on, you are working here. You cannot be relieved." But the man would not accept that decision. He kept going back and agitating the foreman. Finally, the foreman said, "Look, it is out of my hands. Go talk to the superintendent." And so, he went to the superintendent and said, "I have got to go." But the superintendent echoed what the foreman had said, "No, you cannot go. Why do you want to leave, anyway?" The determined man's response was, "I have been called to preach." In desperation one day they finally released him from his job because by this time they were as frustrated as he was. Well, he was gone a few months, then he came back and asked, "Can I have my job back?" Then the superintendent and foreman answered,

"Well, yes you can have your job back, but first of all, we would like an explanation. You would not quit begging to be released from this job because you said you had been called to preach, and we released you so that you could go preach. Now you are back here a few months later wanting your job back. What happened? I thought you said Yahweh called you to preach.

Sheepishly, the man answered, "Well, He did, but after He heard me preach a few times He told me to go back and work in the shipyard!"

When I started out only Yahweh and I believed, and I do not know how many times He wondered about whether or not He had made the right choice. However, no matter how foolish you may feel, you must put the dream into words. You must speak it.

Now, let me tell you what your dream is going to get for you. It is going to get you rejection. Expect that your family is going to reject your dream because, you see, families generally have plans and ambitions for their children. They know what you ought to do and be, and your family is not going to believe what Yahweh put into your heart. Yahshua affirmed that a man's enemies (and that goes for women, too) will be those of his own household. You must be willing to take a stand against Mama and Daddy, against brother and sister, against whomever, if you are going to realize the dream Yahweh puts in your heart.

Whatever dreams your Heavenly Father puts in your heart, declare the dream. Speak it; do not worry about how much it is going to cost. Do not be concerned about how long it is going to take. Just declare the purpose of Yahweh. He will move Heaven and earth to bring His will to pass in your life. Because you see, He delights in those who seek Him. He loves to work for those who honor Him. He is near to all of those who call upon Him. He will reward those who diligently seek Him, and He will never allow you to be confused. He will never allow you to be confounded – if you seek Him with all of your heart. *Pray that you enter not into temptation.* Wait on Yahweh and declare His word.

Declaring the prophetic word will cause people to rise up and reject you but lay hold of the promise. There will be some disappointment but lay hold of the sure word of Yahweh. There will be some distress, and there will probably be long years of preparation, but lay hold of the word of Yahweh. There will be a temptation to go this way, do this thing, and buy that thing, but the word of Yahweh will keep you living a simple lifestyle so that when the word of Yahweh comes to go, you are not encumbered with a lot of things. You are free to move at the voice of Yahweh.

The final step in the seven simple steps to emerging from the desert equipped and enabled is to maintain a simple lifestyle. I believe that the prophetic word of Yahweh will keep you living a simple lifestyle, especially until you understand and know where you are going, and what you are going to do. Then, you can remain flexible. When you are worrying about house payments, car payments, and credit card debit, it is difficult to be flexible. The prophetic word of Yahweh will keep your lifestyle simple. It will cause you to wait on Yahweh's timing.

John had such a prophetic word of Yahweh and kept his life simple. The prophetic word of Yahweh kept John living a simple lifestyle, not because Yahweh was against him having anything nice, but because John knew that he needed to be ready to go. He never knew when the call was coming. He knew what he was called to do. He knew he would not always be in the desert. He knew that one day a call was coming, "Go to Jerusalem. Go. Move now." And when the time came, he was able to move. He could not have moved if he had been living the kind of lifestyle that the world suggested he live, even in his day.

All people have the call of Yahweh on them. Do not just think this instruction is only for pastors or evangelists or those called in the five-fold ministry. Every person born has a call of Yahweh. There is something Yahweh wants to do in your life, and you need that sense of divine calling. You need that prophetic sense because it will help you maintain a simple life. When the Bible says of John that he was clothed with camel's hair and was eating locusts and wild honey, all that means is that he was living a simple lifestyle. Why? Not because that was all he could afford. Not because that was all Yahweh provided. Because

Desert or Wilderness

it is easy to get distracted. It is easy to get off course. The world is always wanting you to do this, that, and the other. But Yahweh wants you to maintain a simple lifestyle so that you are always flexible; you are always mobile; you are not anchored down.

I really believe that people need to be very careful about getting their lives out of order. Sometimes young married couples immediately go into debt. They think just because they have gotten married, they need a new home, a new car, and lot of possessions. You might need to live in a rented apartment. You might need to live in something that does not require you to wait six months to be released from the contract. You might need an older car. When you are obligated six feet over your head, and you are standing on tiptoes, it is difficult to be obedient to the voice of Yahweh. I question whether it is wisdom for pastors (I think the principles apply no matter who you are or what you are called to do) to get involved in trying to buy a house until they know where their ministry is going to be established. It would probably be wiser to rent until they know where their ministry is going to be established. It would probably be wiser to rent until you know where you are going to live permanently. Because we fully support the men who are sent to other cities to pioneer works, those who want to be sent out by this ministry must get their debts where they can live on the same salary as these men who remain on staff here. They probably do not need to be trading automobiles; they probably do not need to be talking to any real estate agents because when the word of Yahweh comes to them, they need to be able to respond in obedience. They do not need to be weighed down with possessions, obligation, and debt. They need to be free to walk out of the desert on short notice. They need to be free to immediately inherit their promised land when their Heavenly Father issues the command, "Go!"

This message I am sharing with you is one I have learned through personal experience. When I have found myself in Yahweh's desert, His preparation place, I have learned to rejoice. I have learned to keep my heart right. I have learned to keep on praying for divine wisdom. I have learned not to turn around, not to change direction. I have learned to wait on my Maker and Redeemer and not quit. I have learned not to let go of the prophetic word of Yahweh to me and to declare the prophetic word in the face of storms. And I have learned to live a simple lifestyle so that when my Heavenly Father calls to me to follow Him into a new dimension, I will be ready to follow. I have learned how to live and live well in the desert places.

If you follow these simple steps that I have learned, you will walk out of the desert one day, and you will be prepared for the next step, the coming journey. You will be ready to inherit the promise.

CONCLUSION

Where are you today? Are you in the wilderness today because you did not pray? I have good news for you. Yahweh meets people in the wilderness. There are angels out there in the wilderness. There are burning bushes in the wilderness. There are voices that speak in the wilderness. There are signs and wonders out there. They are all designed to do one thing and that is to turn you back to faith in Yahweh, to turn you back to waiting on Yahweh.

If you are in Satan's wilderness, repent! Repent. Just say, "Yahweh, I missed a turn in the road. Please show me your will and your way and I will follow you from now on." Do you know what you do when you miss a turn in the road? It does not do any good to go down the road blaming your wife. It will not help you. I never found it would take a mile off the journey. There is only one thing to do when you realize you are wandering around in the wilderness and that is to repent the first chance you get and then when you get to the next crossroad – turn around. There is no need to go on down the road of life fretting and worrying. I did that one time. I was having a good conversation and missed my exit and the next turn around was nineteen miles down the road. I did thirty-eight miles of repenting that day, but I got where I was going because I repented and turned around. And I got out of the wilderness I was in.

Where are you today? Are you in Yahweh's desert place? Are you waiting on Yahweh, being prepared of Yahweh? Rejoice! And be assured, your day is coming. One of these days Yahweh is going to pull you and say, "Look at what I found. Look at what I have been working on. Look at whom I have been preparing."

Now do you understand how important it is to know the difference in being in the desert and being in the wilderness? You see, if you are in the desert, you should not spend your time repenting. What are you repenting of? Are you repenting of your obedience? "Yahweh, I wish I had not listened to you. If I had not listened to you, I would not be out here in the desert."

Six weeks after I got saved, I could have gotten angry and said, "Man, when I got saved, I thought I would get a better job and here I am now without a job." Now, I did not have much religious training, so I went ahead rejoiced when I lost my job. Well, I did not exactly get fired. They left the decision up to me by saying, "You can have a career here or you can quit. And the condition for you having a career here is that you give up this idea about being a preacher. Of course, if you want to hold onto that we will help you make up your mind".

So I decided to hold onto Yahweh and let them do what they wanted to with their job and they let me have my dream and took my job. But that is all right. I rejoiced. Hallelu-Yah! What the Devil thought he was going to turn into a wilderness became a desert place. What looked like a closed door for me became an open door.

Desert or Wilderness

I would not be here today if there not been some closed doors. Now you can get bitter, you can get angry and you can spend the rest of your life blaming somebody for the troubles in your life – or you can learn to turn faith loose. You can learn to turn the confidence of Yahweh loose in that situation and you can say, "This is an open door. Hallelu-Yah! This is an open door." I want to tell you that no matter how dark the circumstance that you may find yourself in, there is an open door.

Every time there appears to be a closed door, look for the open door. Do not worry that you did not get elected to that group. You see, when you are walking under the lordship of Yahshua, guess what? He is in control. When you set your heart to seek righteousness, every decision of your life is being directed from Heaven's throne room. So, you did not go on that trip with all those people. So, you did not get voted in. So, you did not make the team. Guess what? That is an open door. Look for the open door. Do not spend your time crying and bewailing your position, saying, "Yahweh, why do they not like me?" Rest in Yahweh. There is an open door for you. When you have made Yahshua the Messiah, the Savior of your life, there is no person, there is no company, there is no organization, there is no political system that can control your life.

If you are in the military, do not believe for one moment that somebody sitting in a personnel department at a computer who does not even know you will decide where you are sent. Do not believe that. Do not submit to that. Declare that whatever decision is made is coming to you through Yahweh, that the military must get His OK on it. They are not free to do with you what they want to do. They cannot toy around with you. Your life is in the hands of the Creator. Then, when they make a decision that perhaps was not exactly what you wanted to do, do not get shaken. Just remind yourself, "Yahshua is lord of my life. I trust in Yahweh and when doors are closed to me, I will turn, and I will look for the open door."

For there will never be a time in your life when all doors are closed. There may appear to be times in your life when all doors are closed but the door you are looking for may be a trap door. One day you may simply fall through the door and think, "Oh, Yahweh, what has happened to me? I am falling." You are falling right into the middle of the will of Yahweh.

Now I do not believe that Yahweh creates the storms for us. I do not believe that Yahweh turns and fights against us but when we set our face to follow Him, not only can we be assured that His blessing will be added to us, but we can be assured that we are going to come against all the powers of darkness. Every demon in Hell is going to rise up against us to destroy us, to defeat us, to discourage us, to turn us back. Why should it be thought a strange thing if when we set our hearts after Yahshua, the powers of the enemy rise up against us? Have you ever known what it was to break fellowship with a friend? Does that friend take it nicely and say, "It was nice knowing you"? No, what does that friend begin to do? He begins to gossip. First of all, he tries to cajole you. He tries to hold you. He tries to manipulate you. He tries to sway you with sweet words. When I made it known that I was withdrawing from the religious organization I had been in for many years, the first approach was flattery. The first approach was appealing to me. "Oh, we need you. Stay with us. Do not leave us. Stay. Help us change things. Stay and break the rules. Just stay!" But when I would not be swayed when I made it known, in no unmistakable terms, that my heart was fixed on doing what I believed Yahweh had spoken to me to do, those very same people became my enemies. They rose up against me. They spoke against me. Now, before you come to Yahshua, you are in a league with the Devil, with demons, with principalities and powers, and rulers of darkness. The meanest person alive cannot be compared to a little demon in meanness. They know more about meanness, they know more about dirt, they know more about gossip than any human. So why should you ever think that you are going to walk out of the fellowship of darkness and not have those same powers rise up against you? And since spirits can only work through people, they are going to find somebody who will come into agreement with them against you. And the people with whom you have been friends, the people with whom you have been lifelong associates even the members of your own family will turn against you and think they have done Yahweh a favor.

So, what are you going to do? Rejoice! Rejoice! Rejoice! Why? Because you are in a difficult place because of obedience. You see, the fire of persecution becomes like the fire the three young Hebrew men – Hananiah (Shadrach), Mishael (Meshach), and Azariah (Abed-Nego) experienced. If you will keep your heart right, the fire will devour the people who built it and it will never singe a hair on your head. But if you become like them, it will destroy you. So instead of becoming bitter, resentful, and angry and lashing out trying to justify yourself, rejoice and rest in your Heavenly Father. If people do not believe you, they are not going to believe you because you scream louder or protest more. Those who believe you will believe you and those who do not will not be convinced. So do not waste your time trying to convince them, just understand and accept the fact that your obedience to Yahweh has now brought into the light their disobedience. Do not think it a strange thing that obedience brings rejection. Rejoice in it. Rejoice! Everybody will back off and say, "Yahweh's going to get him now. He is going to get him now. Yeah, I knew, I knew, I knew."

People judged that some of the calamities that came into our lives after we withdrew from the religious organization in which we labored were because I left the denomination, an act they viewed as disobedience. BUT MY GOD HAS BEEN FAITHFUL. Yahweh has been so gracious, so good. And I have learned to count it all joy. I have learned that people may interpret some of the happenings that occur in my life as the judgment of Yahweh but I see those same occurrences as the adversary not liking what I have done. And I am telling you, my face is set like a flint. And when I find myself in Yahweh's desert places I am going to walk there with rejoicing in my heart. I am going to count all the days of my kingdom walk as joy. And if I ever find myself in the wilderness again, I am going to repent and repent quickly. I refuse to live in Satan's barren wilderness.

I have been asked if there are any other places besides the desert and the wilderness. Oh, yes. There comes a time when the Heavenly Father says, "Okay, the desert period is finished. Now go do what I have been preparing you to do." Hallelu-Yah! Personally, I feel as if I have been called out of the desert. I feel as if I have been set loosed to do what the Creator prepared me to do.

Nevertheless, sometimes, it seems that Yahweh takes us back into the desert for another preparation period to move up a little higher. Do not despair when that happens. That is our omniscient Father's way. That is His business. Guess what I am going to do when that happens to me? I am going to rejoice and be glad. I am going to keep my heart right. I am certainly not going to be angry with my god. Nor am I going to be out of sorts with myself. I am going to pray for His wisdom and keep on going in the direction I was headed when I found myself in the desert. I am not going to throw in the towel. I am not going to give up my walk of faith. I am going to continue to declare the prophetic word of Yahweh to me no matter what the circumstance may look like. And I am going to live a simple lifestyle. The attitude of my heart will be, *Okay, Daddy, you brought me to your desert, and I know you have something bigger and something better for me to do. I am going to move on with you, Daddy. This next show is going to be great. Hallelu-Yah! The last thing you and I did together was good but this next thing you are preparing me for is going to be great! Praise You, Yahweh! Let Your name be praised in all the earth!*

Floyd Nolan Ball was born on November 14, 1929 in Bothwell, Mississippi. His father, Paul Ball, could not have been prouder and his mother, Ruth, would tell the story of how she held her 12 pound baby up before the Lord and prayed, "Lord, if this boy is not going to serve you, please, just take him." Over the next several years, he began to hear a Voice, first in the plaintive melody and words sung by a Salvation Army group on the street corner of a little Mississippi town: "What Would You Give in Exchange for Your Soul," and then in the spring of 1947 at the age of 17 while attending a revival in a Methodist church, Nolan once again heard that Voice and became aware in his spirit that he was being called to preach. Nolan Ball answered that call and faithfully served the Lord up until his last day on June 19, 2018, when he passed away at the age of 88.

After graduating from Baldwin County High School, Nolan served four years in the U.S. Air Force, attaining the rank of Sergeant before his honorable discharge in 1951. That same year, he met and married Shirley Navello from London, England and in 1953, Nolan and Shirley made the choice to submit their lives to God at First Assembly of God in Alexandria, Virginia. In 1954, they started a family and moved to Lakeland, Florida, where Nolan enrolled at Southeastern Bible College of the Assemblies of God. They lived in Lakeland for six years where Nolan attended classes and worked to provide for his growing family. He was Valedictorian at Southeastern College, giving the commencement address at his graduation in 1957. He also graduated from Florida Southern College in 1958 with honors. From 1957-1986, Pastor Ball led Assembly of God churches in Lakeland FL, Angel City FL, Talladega AL, Tallahassee FL, and Panama City FL. He served as both a District Presbyter in the Alabama and West Florida Districts of the Assemblies of God and as a General Council Presbyter from the West Florida District.

There were many pivotal moments in the life of Nolan Ball, but perhaps the most determinative point in time was in the early summer of 1969 when he was selected to become the tenth pastor of what was then known as Dirego Park Assembly of God (now known as The Rock.) He moved to Panama City with his wife, Shirley, and their children and quickly set about the work of the ministry, building not only a new worship facility and gymnasium, but also laying the foundation for the Kingdom House that was destined to be built in Bay County. And although he may not have known it then, every step on the road that led Nolan and Shirley to this beautiful forgotten coast, had prepared them for the life they would lead and the mark they would make.

Nolan Ball was an Apostle of Christ whose voice rang out through Bay County for 48 years. It rang in a move of Holy Ghost that swells and vibrates with supernatural power to this day, sounding a call to hear and follow The Voice. During those 48 years, as a spiritual father, Apostle Ball established 26 men in the ministry, beginning in 1987 and ending in 2018. Along with establishing men in the U.S., he has worked with national leaders in Peru, South America; Jamaica, West Indies; Kenya, East Africa, and Zaire, West Africa to establish churches. He gave himself completely to these men, just as he had always given himself completely to his every calling.

Nolan Ball loved the ministry. He remained committed to the will and purpose of Yahweh as leader of The Rock of Panama City until his retirement in January 2018. His leadership opened wide the gates for thousands of people to be changed from glory to glory. With Christ as the Chief Cornerstone, Apostle Ball had successfully laid the foundation upon which the next generation could build.

www.ingramcontent.com/pod-product-compliance
Lightning Source LLC
Chambersburg PA
CBHW072027110526
44592CB00012B/1422